WILLING TO ENGAGE

Thank you!

Larry Vosen

WILLING TO ENGAGE

SILENT NO MORE!

Lawrence T. (Larry) Vosen, Ph.D.

WILLING TO ENGAGE

SILENT NO MORE!

Copyright © 2012

Lawrence T. (Larry) Vosen
Las Vegas, NV

First Edition

Library of Congress Cataloging-in-Publication Data Assignment Number: 2012908072

The 7th Column Movement™

ISBN-13: 978-1475095692
ISBN-10: 1475095694

Imprint: Las Vegas, NV
CreateSpace, North Charleston, SC

PROLOGUE

Ever since the publication of my memoir, "A Diamond on The Wall", I have been asked to provide the explanation I offered at The Vietnam Veteran's Memorial Wall (in the summer of 2011), when questions were asked about, "Why so young?" and "School and Home". Although the memoir is an accurate presentation of my near eighteen month tour of duty in Vietnam, questions are now being asked about why I signed a "Letter of Intent to Enlist in the Army" at 16, and why I physically entered the Service at 17. I have also been asked to provide more information about my family and childhood, because the statement made in that earlier writing, that "Things had been tough between my mom and me during my last couple of years at home", conflicts with the happy and joyous times I wrote about, requiring some sort of explanation. Finally, a lot of people want to know exactly how much money I had "stashed away" while I was winning so prolifically at poker during that time.

While it is true that my youth, like the youth of many others, was strewn with landmines, and laden with distressing events, I did have a joyous and loving childhood. Things happen outside the family circle though, that can impact a child in positive or negative ways. In my teen years I experienced some negative outside influences, and through those experiences learned the importance of maintaining and enforcing the value of each individual. Destroying another's self-worth is an easy task at times, which makes it even more essential that we <u>realize how absolutely valuable and essential each of you are as a person, and how critical your involvement within this world truly is</u>. Beyond our wildest imaginings, we have worth, and that worth cannot be judged or diminished by anyone other than you (and our Creator). In my early years I learned that only you can permit your worth to be diminished by others.

My mother, the very one responsible for teaching me this truth, forgot for a while, and in the forgetting, we grew apart!

With regard to the age of my enlistment, I am compelled to state that contrary to popular opinion, dysfunctional families are not new! Bullying, teasing and tormenting are not new! Abuses, whether physical, sexual, or psychological, are not new! Feelings of uselessness, inadequacy and ineptness are not new! These matters have been with us from the moment we got kicked out of the Garden of Eden, and we are told that, "Cain rose up against Abel his brother and killed him" (Genesis 4:8 ENB). And, these matters will be with us throughout the remainder of our time on this planet (until Messiah returns). With these truths at my base, I will seek to explain the unusual and drastic alternatives I chose.

Furthermore, I fervently concede that my personal experiences force me to rebel at the notion that the world has "changed so radically" from when I was young; rebel at the thought that the troubles we now experience are directly related to those radical changes. I could not disagree more! Therefore, I challenge you to read this book, and then tell me that at the core of the matter, things on a personal, emotional and individual level have in fact "radically changed". My resounding reply will be, "Nothing is new!"

The troubles we are experiencing internationally today are directly related to the fact that a very "silent majority" of people, throughout the world, have grown complacent or fearful, and have surrendered their will and rights to a very "vocal minority" of political extremists, liars and bullies. The silence of that majority is allowing outrageous social and political agendas to be implemented unhindered within our societies and governments.

Aside from that silence though, the primary "social" differences we see in the world today lie in the realities of two truthful facts: First, everything is magnified in our sight today, because the population of the world has been so enormously magnified. In 1950, for instance, the world population was about 2.5 billion. Today, the population exceeds 7 billion, and it is growing exponentially.

The second fact is related to technology, and specifically deals with the speed of communications. Once you couple the size of our population today, with the speed and manner in which we learn about things happening within that population, you will realize that these are the only significant differences between the way people acted throughout the 1950's and early 1960's, and what we think we see and know to be true today. **And yes, by that I am saying, what we see and hear today is being manipulated.**

It is vital, therefore, that I begin this book by telling you, no matter how young or how old you are, no matter what you are doing, or where you are: in school, in a retirement home, or somewhere in between; working or unemployed; an executive or a laborer; a professional or a beggar, this book is not about your station in life, or about your financial worth. This book is about you, and about your incredible value as a person, and about how a very vocal minority is trying to diminish your value and self-worth.

Second, this book is not designed to merely make you feel good about yourself. While I am striving to prove your value and worth, with regard to who and what you are, it is not my intent to simply make you feel warm and fuzzy. The intent of this book is to motivate you to engage in the battle for the whole of society (one person at a time). This engagement issue is urgent too, because unless we speak out now, and stop the nonsense surrounding us, we will lose our voice entirely in a short time, and society, as we know it, will be altered forevermore.

I also pray to offer hope to millions of children, teenagers and young adults who think they are alone, and do not believe anyone in my generation understands them. We understand! Many of us went through it! And many are willing to help today.

Furthermore, I want to offer hope to parents feeling overwhelmed by everything happening in our world. We need not be overwhelmed. We can take control again. We can make a difference. The bottom line though, is we have to want to take control. We have to want to make a difference. And in the wanting, we must be willing to engage against those who want to steal that hope from us!

From the foundation surrounding the joy and love of my childhood, the chapters entitled, "My Tumultuous Years", will show how life unraveled for me. The events detailed were mostly out of my control. I will also show how those events impacted my family too, because it is important for parents and children today to know that regardless of the magnificence of any person's particular childhood, bad things can still happen.

In context, then, "A Diamond on the Wall" speaks toward personal success rising from the depths of despair, while this book, "Willing To Engage", shows that despair can come from successful and joyous beginnings, and that even the best intentions and efforts of a parent, child, or concerned citizen, may often end in seemingly utter failure. Together, then, both books present the fact that we must never give up on ourselves, or our children (or parents), and that successful endings can result from the fact that someone did not give up. Successful endings result because someone is willing to engage!

Lest we get confused in this area, I also believe that "tough love" is crucial to not giving-up! Our willingness to engage must include radical changes or alterations in the manner in which we deal with our children, parents, siblings, spouses, or anyone else, when the destructive nature of their actions become injurious. Co-dependency cycles are vicious and destructive, and tough love must be used to break those damaging cycles. Being willing to engage includes taking stern measures to protect yourself and your loved ones.

Suicide is the third leading cause of death for the age group, 13-24, behind accidental injury and homicide. The age is getting lower every year, and the percentage of suicide is increasing. It is my fervent hope, that telling the remainder of my story will stop someone from ending their life, or the lives of others. Too many people are surrendering all hope, because they see no future, because they are caught up in horrible circumstances, and see no out but death.

During my tumultuous years I experienced and knew their pain. In many ways, my memories force me to share their pain today. No matter the depth of despair though, there is always an out; always a solution; always hope; always people and places to turn for an assist! I knew these things then, and I feel compelled to extend a hand of hope through these pages today.

Additionally, this book is a wake-up-call for the personal involvement and participation of every citizen, including today's youth. Together we must labor to set aright the deplorable condition of our world. Together, young and old must put forth an effort to stop the insanity that is causing such dismay (socially and politically). Together, we can make great strides, but we must be willing to engage in order to accomplish the much needed results.

Life is short and difficult enough. There are common sense solutions to our problems. First, we need to reconnect as families, and as a society. We must learn to laugh again too, in sincere respect and true love. There is tremendous healing power in a good, shared, belly laugh with people we know are seeking our well-being. I hope to bring laughter to your heart as you discover the respect and regard which this person has for you! Your personal well-being is my primary concern, and lightening your load is my intent!

Therefore, these pages reflect the profound lessons I learned between my entry into the ninth grade and my honorable discharge from the Army before my 20th birthday. These lessons, however, have taken a lifetime for me to learn to express. The matters discussed will also show how our silence and unwillingness to engage is negatively impacting our lives today.

With all my heart, mind and soul, I pray that you find these expressions worthwhile, because, aside from my faith, these things are at the very foundation of my life, and abide within the core of my being. I believe they may be the foundation needed to help heal our sick and dying society.

Sincerely,

Larry Vosen

(Joey Junior Bones)

Let us not seek perfection,
because we are not perfect.
Let us not judge,
because we are not gods.
Let us not dictate,
because we are not tyrants.
We are Human...
We Learn...
We Fall...
We Fail...
We Get Up...
We Reach Out...
We Help...
We Live...
We Conquer...
We Let Go...
But,
We Never GIVE UP!

GLOSSARY I
POLITICAL DEFINITIONS:

Glossaries are traditionally placed at the back of books. I am placing these definitions here, however, because I am hoping this book will appeal to a variety of age groups. Unless each generation knows the true definition of these significant words, however, we may very well discover our nation, as was originally designed, no longer exists.

I am using these particular words within this book exactly as defined here.

The following three definitions have been provided by Wikipedia at:
http://www.wikipedia.org

- A **democratic republic** is a country which is both a republic and a democracy.

- **Democracy** is an egalitarian form of government in which all the citizens of a nation together determine public policy, the laws and the actions of their state, requiring that all citizens (meeting certain qualifications) have an equal opportunity to express their opinion. In practice, "democracy" is the extent to which a given system approximates this ideal, and a given political system is referred to as "a democracy" if it allows a certain approximation to ideal democracy. Although no country has ever granted all its citizens (i.e. including minors) the vote, most countries today hold regular elections based on egalitarian principles, at least in theory.

- A **Republic** is a form of government in which the government is officially apportioned to the control of the people, or a significant portion of which, and where offices of state are subsequently directly or indirectly elected or appointed. In modern times, a common simplified definition of a republic is a government where the head of state is not a monarch. The word *republic* is derived from the Latin phrase *res publica*, which can be translated as "the public affair", and often used to describe a state using this form of government.

The following three definitions are provided by Asker:

- **Communism** is similar, except that communism (IN THEORY) is governed by the people, for the people. So, communism combines socialist theories of economics with political control. In communism, the role of the Communist Party is central, and it controls most aspects of society. Even motorcycle clubs are run by the Party. It is supposedly class-less, with everyone being equal, and all property being owned by everyone collectively, not by individuals. Karl Marx saw it as the ideal and inevitable system, but every effort to implement it has failed, at least partially because almost all people are generally self-interested and greedy most of the time.

- **Socialism** is an economic system. It uses government ownership of the means of production (e.g., factories) to direct the economy. It uses social welfare programs to promote universal employment, health care, and pensions. It is practiced, in limited form, as "social democracy" in much of Europe, which is part free-market economy (companies directing production by determining customer wants and supply and demand) and part state-run (mass transit [airlines, buses, trains], some critical industries). Socialism does not have to be democratic, though. Socialism is also very broad: some socialists want to nationalize all major businesses, some want to nationalize just a few. So, socialism is more a set of economic theories than a single ideology.

- **Totalitarianism** is a political system. In totalitarianism, the government is undemocratic in the extreme: it is a total dictatorship. Totalitarian states have a powerful secret police, no protection of individual rights, a leader who rules without political challenge in elections or serious political restraints of any kind, and similar traits. However, some normal authoritarian dictatorships have these characteristics. What makes a totalitarian government unique is ideology. The government wants to actively reshape the minds of the population, to make them follow a certain cause and believe in a certain way, changing the very nature of society. Totalitarianism, according to political scientists, is very rare. It existed in the Soviet Union for a time, but ideology became less important to the Soviets after Stalin died, so the USSR stopped being totalitarian. Nazi Germany is the other classic example of a totalitarian government.

So, communism, with its notion that the Party is part of everything, lends itself to totalitarianism, but not all communist countries are totalitarian. Likewise, not all totalitarian countries are communist: the Nazis were generally capitalists, but their absolute dictatorship and ideology made them totalitarian. **Socialism and communism are much related. Both see the means of production as being owned by the public, not by private companies. Both try to create an egalitarian, class-less society, where the poor are given more and the rich are given less, so that everyone is closer to being equal.** Communism is simply more communal -- with nobody owning private property -- and emphasizes the importance of the Communist Party as the embodiment of the will of the people.

In understanding these six words, I am asking the people of America to decide which form of Government they want in place for our future, because the outcome of every election, as well as the judicial and civic appointments made by those we elect, have and will determine the very nature of our country. This is especially true for the elections taking place in November of 2012. And if you think your vote does not count, then you have just reduced yourself to zero.

(Thomas Jefferson)

"The democracy will cease to exist when you take away from those who are willing to work and give to those who would not."

(John Adams)

"Democracy... while it lasts is more bloody than either aristocracy or monarchy. Remember, democracy never lasts long. It soon wastes, exhausts, and murders itself. There is never a democracy that did not commit suicide."

(John Adams)

"The right of a nation to kill a tyrant in case of necessity can no more be doubted than to hang a robber, or kill a flea."

GLOSSARY II

COMMON WORDS USED THROUGHOUT WILLING TO ENGAGE:

As in Glossary I, it is important for each reader to know the intent of my word usage, especially as applied to these very significant words. This is especially true, because the manner in which we use words today is changing. The last thing I want is to think that we may not be speaking the same language. This glossary is offered, therefore, to insure a common understanding for these particular words. It would be a shame for the intent of this message to be lost.

(All but one definition is according to Random House Webster's College Dictionary. The word, Humility – is derived from the root word used in Hebrew and Greek):

- **Appreciate**: To value or regard highly; place a high estimate on. To be grateful or thankful for. To be fully conscious of; be aware of; detect. To raise in value. To increase in value.

- **Dignity**: Bearing, conduct, or manner indicative of self-respect, formality, or gravity. Nobility or elevation or character; worthiness.

- **Engage:** Involved in or committed to something, as a political cause. To occupy the attention or efforts of; involve. To enter into conflict with. To assume an obligation.

- **Esteem**: To regard highly or favorably; regard with respect or admiration. To consider as of a certain value or a certain type; regard. Favorable opinion or judgment; respect or regard; to hold a person in esteem.

- **Honor**: Honesty, fairness, or integrity in one's beliefs and actions: a code of honor. A source of credit or distinction. High respect: as for worth, merit, or rank. Upright. Credible. Good reputation. Dignity.

- **Humility**: At its base, humility means to have a correct estimation of oneself. To NOT think more highly or lowly than one actually is. (This definition is Not Webster's, but emanates from a study of the root of this word, from both Hebrew and Greek).

- **Instinct**: A natural or innate impulse, inclination, or tendency.

- **Integrity**: Uncompromising adherence to moral and ethical principles; soundness of moral character; honesty. The state of being whole or entire. A sound or unimpaired condition.

- **Justice**: The quality of being just; righteousness, equitableness, or moral rightness. Rightfulness or lawfulness. The quality of being true or correct. The moral principle determining just conduct.

- **Moderation:** The quality of being moderate.
    Moderate: Kept or keeping within reasonable limits; not extreme, excessive, or intense. Opposed to extreme views or actions.

- **Righteous – ness**: Characterized by uprightness or morality. Morally right or justifiable. Acting in a moral or upright way; virtuous.

- **Self-worth**: The sense of one's own value or worth as a person; self-esteem; self-respect.
    Self-esteem: Self-respect.
    Self-respect: Proper esteem or regard for the dignity of one's character.

- **Tumult**: Violent and noisy commotion or disturbance of a crowd or mob; uproar. A general outbreak, riot, uprising, or other disorder. Highly distressing agitation of mind or feeling; turbulent mental or emotional disturbance.

- **Tumultuous**: Full of tumult or riotousness; uproarious; disorderly. Highly agitated; distraught; turbulent.

- **Value**: Relative worth or importance. Magnitude, quantity. Favorable regard. Often, values; the abstract concepts of what is right, worthwhile, or desirable; principles or standards. Any object or quality desirable as a means or as an end in itself. To consider with respect to worth or importance. To esteem. See Appreciate.

TABLE OF CONTENTS

Pledge of Allegiance

I pledge allegiance to the flag of the United States of America, and to the republic for which it stands, one nation under God, indivisible, with liberty and justice for all.

Introduction – Entrusted With a Coin

L et me begin exposing the things I wish to express, by offering the first "philosophical" lesson I ever learned as a youngster. I did not know this was philosophical back then, I just thought it seemed right. It seemed as the basis for a good way to look at people, because I think this is the way I always hoped people would look at me.

Simply stated, I believe every person on this planet (past, present or future) is (or will be) entrusted with at least one gift, ability or talent. Everybody has at least one thing to offer, and because no two people are alike, the gift, ability, or talent they each possess, is unique within the world! For ease of reference, I have always called that gift, ability or talent, "a coin", or "our coin", or "their coin".

Throughout most of my life I have believed this premise, and because of that belief, I have sincerely tried to live my life accordingly, and treat others with the respect that demands. Being human, I have not always been successful!

Personal failures aside, it does not matter what our particular gift or talent is. Not every person is meant to speak before throngs as they offer spectacular speeches. Not every person is meant to throw 94 MPH fastballs as major league pitchers. Not every person is meant to be a doctor or a nurse, or whatever position of importance or significance you might want to name. Every person on this planet, however, is unique, and in that uniqueness, each one is gifted differently. And that, if you can accept it, is a very cool thing.

The significant truth to this, however, lies in the matter of whether we use our coin or not. Unused, the coin is useless. Used properly though, the coins become very valuable. And that is my first "philosophical" lesson!

Allow me to offer a few examples:

If, for instance, you have the ability to bring joy to someone's life by merely sitting and talking with a person, even if only once in a while, but you refuse to use that ability, then you have buried your coin, abused your gift, and it is all useless. Does that make sense?

The interesting thing about using our gift or talent, however, is it really makes us happy. What makes you feel happy and fulfilled?

If you can answer that question, then that is the thing you should strive to do as often as possible. In the ninth grade I discovered what it was that really brought me joy, but it all got lost for many years, because I simply did not understand what I had discovered. Sad as that is, I know that is happening in many lives today. If we become willing to engage though, I believe we can remedy that. We can learn our purpose, be happy, and in the process, bring happiness into the lives of others.

I am certain we all know people who purchase something they have wanted for a long time, and are ecstatic. They take great joy in the care, maintenance and mere appreciation of whatever they bought. But the true happiness those people receive through their purchase, comes in the sharing (or even showing-off) of that thing. Possessing something is one thing; sharing that thing with others is where the joy really does set in.

A perfect example is the big "Automobile Auctions" taking place around the world. There are people who love restoring vintage automobiles. The greater the restoration required – the greater is the satisfaction in seeing the fully restored vehicle. But the real joy comes in sharing the fullness of the restoration with other people. It's true!

In the sharing, "before" and "after" photographs are examined. Minute details of the restoration process are itemized and noted. They will go as far as to lie on the ground to show off the beauty of the underside of the restored vehicle. Such is their pride in what has been done.

The gift the person might possess may be in their ability to actually restore a vintage vehicle, but the true joy for them comes when an opportunity presents itself to share the restoration with another enthusiast. The value of the coin is in the sharing! The remainder of the time, the restored vehicle sits in a garage and is viewed solely by the restorer. Eventually, the initial joy may wear off, and many of those restored vehicles are sold, which allows for other restoration projects. The joy, in either case, is in the sharing! Such is the use or misuse of our coins.

Now, in case you have not seen it yet in my writings, I refer to myself as "outgoing", or "loud", or "unreserved", or "bold", and in all honesty, I am very thankful for the fact that I am a naturally (and normally) very friendly sort of person. And in that friendliness, I have an ability to talk openly with people without too much fear.

Oh, I know that I am not the most interesting guy in the world to chat with. The ability I have been given though, to talk openly without fear, somehow allows me to penetrate into people's hearts, and allows them to either relax, or allows them to reveal something about themselves they normally would hide. Somehow, through these exchanges, I can visually see a broader smile on some faces, or see shoulders sag just a bit less, as some pressure is released. I love that!

Accompanying this ability, (the flip-side to my coin), is an innate desire to make people feel better about who they are; to uphold them; to increase their self-esteem; to coach or mentor in order to strengthen. I truly love doing that!

Understanding my coin, you can imagine how painful and distressing it is for me, to see so many people ignoring their gifts and keeping their coins hidden in their pockets. Somehow, somewhere, too many people have been told they are useless, and have no value. Thinking this true, many people with wonderful gifts have been silenced.

Furthermore, I think we have allowed ourselves to believe that 21st Century life is more difficult than it is, and that "matters of this world" are beyond our ability to comprehend and understand.

3

Adding to the insult is the notion we frequently hear, that because of the complexity of the "matters of this world", we need to surrender our thought processes to those better suited and trained.

WHAT RUBBISH!

What matters, what is truly important, is that you honestly evaluate your life, and recognize that we all labor at something. And the two-part question we must ask ourselves in that evaluation process is, "Am I doing the best I can, at whatever it is I am laboring at, and do I value or dismiss the people with whom I might be interacting?" If you cannot answer that question positively and favorably, then you are hiding your coin!

If you are hiding your coin in the belief that you are incapable of understanding the complex nature of life today, or if you have simply stopped trying to make a difference, then, to be blunt, you have surrendered your voice and devalued yourself to zero in all areas. Your coin is of no worth – either to you, or the world.

How sad is that?

The simple truth to all of this though, is I have never met a zero, and I am willing to wager that you have never met a zero either.

No matter who I talk or interact with, every person I have met throughout my life has had the capacity to offer something. In presenting a smile, a nod, or even a door held open, we offer value to those we meet, because in doing even the smallest thing, we are recognizing another individual as worthy. And through that recognition we not only use our coin, we give value to them as well. At a minimum I strive to do these small things, and I see the impact my efforts have on others. You are capable of doing this too!

This book, therefore, is meant to prove that value exists where some see a deficit or waste, and this writing is as much about individual commitment and self-worth, as it is about family and society. This is so, because the manner in which we value ourselves, and the manner in which we use our coins, as we interact with others, ultimately determines the full and true value of that coin.

At sixteen I knew I had value, but I had no way to prove or maintain what I knew to be true. <u>So, I personally made the changes needed in my life!</u>

As I have said many times, "I did not know how to back down, so I plowed through". In doing so, I survived. This book is offered to all who have given-up, or who are about to give up. And, it is forcibly presented, because if we continue backing down, we will lose our individual and collective liberties and freedoms, for which so many have sacrificed and died.

Further, this book is offered as a starting point in a challenge for sensible change. When I began making my notes for this work, I thought it possible to touch on my tumultuous years without expanding on how those years impacted my adult life. But as the words unfolded, the person I have become, and what I believe and stand for, has all sort of spilled out in a controlled convulsion. Beginning with some fond childhood memories, my mind transitioned to a very ugly period in my life, and then moved to the fact that I was willing to make radical changes in order to maintain my personal identity.

This book, therefore, transitions in three stages, and within those transitions you will see how profound my sentiments with regard to personal self-worth are; how intense my desire to instill value and confidence is; and how willing to engage I remain today in defense of what is right, proper, and fitting; in defense of integrity, fairness, justice and truth. Paralleling the transitions of my life, I know that sensible change requires a willingness to engage in order to maintain our personal and national identity. My hope is that through all of these things you too will realize that we must become willing to engage in order to maintain these things as well.

Admittedly, I detest the direction that we, as a society, are headed. I detest the narcissistic attitude that is so pervasive. I detest the notion that we must pander to the weaknesses, indulgences and often appalling behavior of individuals who are unwilling to do anything for themselves; who are unwilling to contribute to the betterment of their own lives, let alone bettering society.

This is one example of how we are backing down today:

First, through a very long-running devaluation process, too many people now believe they are worthless, unwanted and unnecessary. This is evidenced by the fact that more and more people are in despair, and depression is rampant. Further, a growing number of people are sad, troubled and distressed in their feelings of helplessness and uselessness, and it all culminates in the reality that suicide, especially childhood and young adult suicide rates, are skyrocketing.

Let us then add to the mix of those truths, a very vocal minority of special interest groups, and their experts, insisting we all tolerate and pander to people who choose to lead meaningless and non-productive lifestyles. The supposed "experts" also say we must financially support these people.

Conclusion: Many with value are declared worthless, while the self-declared worthless are subsidized instead of motivated.

How ignorant is that?

In our world today, we have a very vocal minority who insist that the achievers must pay for the maintenance and upkeep of the underachievers and non-achievers, whether they _ever_ attempt to improve their lives or not. Adding insult to injury, we require nothing in return from them; we require absolutely no contribution back to society.

As evidence of our backing down, the silent majority, who traditionally DO possess higher levels of integrity, and moral standards, sits idly by and permits this nonsense to continue!

Whatever happened to self-worth? Whatever happened to contributing to the good of society? Whatever happened to simple folks, working hard in order to live good and decent lives, without the government interfering in, or with, those lives? Where is the value in what we are doing? And what are we teaching the next generations if we allow this pandering to continue?

I knew I had self-worth, because I was raised with self-worth. Whenever anyone tried to diminish that self-worth, I fought back. This book, therefore, is about reinforcing the fact that we each have value, and if anyone ever tries to diminish our value, we must fight back; fight HARD if needed. We each have value, and only we can surrender that – no one can take it from us.

I fought hard back then, and I am willing to fight hard again today. Maybe together we can truly accomplish something positive. Shall we try?

***

I have labored in my Prologue and Introduction to help you know who I am, and what I am about, because this book will be considered radical by some. I have provided the above information in an attempt to present a firm image of the real me, because in that knowledge this message gains meaning. I also labored under the notion that anyone reading "A Diamond on The Wall", and "The Letters of Faith", along with this book, would know precisely who and what I am, as well as where I 'stand' on many issues!

In the knowledge of these things though, I was asked a couple of questions by Charlie (my wife of 41 years), and in the asking of those questions I was confronted with some eye-opening realities…

Charlie, who was raised in an orphanage until she was 14, could not grasp how I could say, "To the core of my being, I knew I had value." She also asked, "How did you know you had self-worth?" Furthermore, "What do you mean by value and self-worth?"

Wow!

As I shared these questions with my other "Editors", I heard, "What gave you the instinct to believe you could succeed in whatever you tried?" And finally, "What propelled you to get off the floor and fight back?"

WOW!

Although I have taught and lectured about these topics in many ways throughout my adult life, I cannot recall ever being asked such base and vital questions. Charlie has heard most of my reflective thoughts many times over the years, yet even through the use of those stories, and any number of other tools, I have never before been asked questions of such depth. I hope my reply is satisfactory:

In "A Diamond on The Wall", I spoke about my waking at 4:00 AM on Saturday's (from the age of four) to be with my dad while we shopped to restock the delicatessen. Further, I also talked about spending eight years attending the same elementary school. Within these two facts lies a great deal of untold information.

On those Saturday's that I spent with my dad, I watched and listened, as he always affirmed and uplifted the people he talked with. He uplifted and affirmed me too. Dad, and mom as well, encouraged Fred and me, in whatever we did, repeatedly telling us, "You can do it!" And, especially when we were doing our chores and helping around the store and house, we were always shown and told how much our effort and contribution was appreciated. Our value, self-worth and confidence were uplifted and affirmed every day as we labored with our parents, or played whatever sport was in season.

Add to this then, the fact that my brother Fred and I walked to school every day. Fred, being two years older, held my hand as we walked to school that first year. We did not go home for lunch though. For eight years our mom packed lunches for us every day. Significant here is the fact that when she packed our daily lunches, our mom used to write a note on the napkins that always accompanied our lunch. In those notes she would offer simple quotes, poems or thoughts of the day, and those notes always had an uplifting, affirming, confidence building, value establishing, or self-worth acknowledging message at their core!

From the time we learned to read we were provided a daily affirmation to the fact that we had value and self-worth. Fred and I both were taught about honor, integrity, humility, and dignity, throughout our elementary school years, and the messages were backed-up by verbal affirmations as we interacted with our parents throughout those years.

Finally, in response to, "What propelled you to get off the floor and fight back?" I will offer the following thought:

I played football, baseball and basketball from the time I was in 2nd grade. At the same time, Fred and I were being taught, and encouraged, to win in whatever we did, whether playing cards, or out on the field competing. We did not compete to lose! Additionally, organized sports taught me some very basic instincts with regard to competition. When I was knocked to the floor, my instinctive reaction was to get back up. When I was pushed, my instinctive reaction was to push back – harder! When I was hit, my instinctive reaction was to hit back, with as much force as I could muster! NOT DIRTIER, just harder.

I truly believe this sort of interaction and discipline is sorely missing in today's society. I know that Charlie never received these affirmations as a child. I know a lot of kids, and adults too, who never received these sorts of encouragements. But Fred and I did receive these uplifting messages every day. If we fouled-up, it was the mistake that was addressed, not our personal value or self-worth. We never heard, "You are stupid", but we did hear, "Well, that was pretty stupid." And there is a huge difference between the two.

In the knowledge of these things, I am writing "Willing To Engage", not only as a wake-up-call, but as a source of affirmation and encouragement to those who have never known the fullness of their value and self-worth. In case you have never been told, and as you will be reminded throughout these pages, YOU have tremendous value! YOU have inestimable worth!

NAPKIN MESSAGES!

(Billy Graham)
"Courage is contagious. When a brave man takes
a stand, the spines of others are stiffened."

(Henry Wadsworth Longfellow)
"In character, in manners, in all things,
the supreme excellence is simplicity."

(Abraham Lincoln)
"Character is like a tree and reputation like a shadow.
The shadow is what we think of it; the tree is the real thing."

(Ralph Waldo Emerson)
"God does not intend us all to be rich, or powerful
or great, but He does intend us all to be friends."

(Albert Schweitzer)
"One thing I know: the only ones among you who will be
really happy are those who have sought and found how to serve."

(John Wayne)
"Courage is being scared to death-
but saddling up anyway."

(Robert Louis Stevenson)
"Don't judge each day by the harvest you reap,
but by the seeds that you plant."

Chapter 1 – Childhood Memories, Part I

When I think of my childhood, I cannot help but recall some of the beauty and purity of it all, because until I entered high school, I grew-up in an atmosphere of nurturing, compassion, encouragement, and genuine love. And through all of those positive things, I knew I had self-worth. In "A Diamond on The Wall" I spoke often of my mother's illnesses and frequent, lengthy trips to the hospital, and the reality of her poor health weighed heavily on us all. Financially, my parents were in ruin, yet even in that ruin little miracles kept happening (when things were their most bleak), which always "lifted and lightened the load". Times of trial and testing were always present, but throughout it all I can sincerely say that until November, 1965, no one in my family ever mistreated me. Mine was a childhood of wonderful memories, which helped me push through those tumultuous years.

In preparation for these chapters on my childhood, I considered presenting a running narrative, or chronological telling, of the memorable events that took place as I grew-up, so you could catch a glimpse of the full spectrum of joy and love we shared. But as I wrote about such events, I didn't think anyone would really care about that stuff. As wonderful as my family might have been, and as memorable as many of those notable events are, they did not add to your self-worth, or contribute to your value. Nor did they stress the urgent need for us all to engage today in matters related to our society, nation, and world.

Nonetheless, I cannot leave huge holes in the telling of these things either, because then the questions emanating through, "A Diamond on The Wall" will not be answered. Further, without offering some glimpse into the joy and love of my childhood, the full impact of my tumultuous years would be lost, and in the loss of that flavor, you might never see the despair, or the victory.

Because of these things, I wish to tell you a few stories from that time, and show how the firm foundation was laid early, which helped me determine the path I needed to walk as I "came of age". I sincerely hope the stories I have chosen will impact your funny bone and cause some laughter, or even cause some tears, because such was the fullness of my youth.

To begin then, my story must start with the fact that all four of my grandparents were born, "In the Old Country". My dad's folks (Paternal Grandparents) were European. My grandfather, being Jewish – was born and raised in Germany, and my grandmother, being Catholic – was born and raised in Croatia. I do not know when grandma came to the United States. My grandfather and his brother, Ben, however, left Germany before the outbreak of World War I, because they refused to serve in the Kaiser's army. My paternal grandparents met in Milwaukee, while my grandfather was a chef at The Hotel Milwaukee. They settled in Cleveland, Ohio sometime in the early 1920's. Grandma and grandpa had three sons: Herman, Fred (my dad), and Adolph (Rusty).

My mother's folks (Maternal Grandparents) are both from Lebanon; she from south of Beirut, and he from northern Lebanon, somewhere outside of Tripoli. Both were Catholic. In Lebanese, grandmother is "Situ", and grandfather is "Jiddu". My Situ and Jiddu met in Cleveland in the early 1900's, and to the best of my knowledge they had some fourteen children. The mortality rate was horrible back then though, so only five of their children survived, and had children of their own. The five surviving children were: Mary, Louise, Loretta, Laurice (my mom) and Raymond.

The families ultimately met and became rooted together, through a place known as The Hickory Steak House – the restaurant owned by "Mr. V", my "Master Chef" paternal grandfather. The Hickory House opened in 1927, and was in operation under that name until he retired in 1960. To the best of our knowledge, nine (9) marriages resulted because of relationships begun at the restaurant. Naturally, that is where my mom and dad met.

My brother, Fred, was born in January of 1947, and I was born in December of 1948. For the most part, before the age of five, we lived in "The Big House" on the Eastside of Cleveland, with my paternal grandparents. We moved in the spring of my 4th year.

In "A Diamond on The Wall" I mentioned that my dad was in an automobile accident when I was two years old, and that that event was my first solid memory. I recall earlier events, but this is where my memory begins in earnest.

Nonetheless, glass shards remained in dad's head after the accident, and along with the concussion he suffered, and any number of other after effects, my father would fall asleep, or get extremely drowsy, whenever the sunlight hit his head as he was driving. By the time I was four, these symptoms had gotten so bad that dad had to stop working as a delivery driver. That is when mom and dad went into business for themselves, purchasing (leasing) a nice-sized grocery store / delicatessen at 4702 Storer Avenue, on the Westside of Cleveland. They named the business, F & L Delicatessen, and we lived in the house behind the store for almost seven years.

Between the time of my Dad's accident, and our move to the store though, three noteworthy events remain in my memory, which summarize the relationship I had back then with my brother.

It must be noted, however, that I am a snooper. I love getting into things and investigating. I love playing. I did not care one bit about getting dirty or remaining clean. Fred, on the other hand, was meticulous. In everything he did, Freddy-boy (as he was nick-named and called by the whole family throughout our early years) was an ideal child. I say that to him teasingly today, and he readily admits the truth of the matter: he was nearly-perfect, while I was a trouble-some rogue. I was always into something, while Fred always seemed to maintain a clean and almost impeccable manner about him.

Aside from being the oldest grandchild, Fred was also a "miracle baby", because (as a carryover from her bout with polio), our mother was not supposed to have been able to carry any children. Those two things, along with his cleanliness, led Fred to be heavily favored by my grandmother.

13

Grandma would dress up Fred and take him everywhere. He went shopping downtown with her all the time, while I was content snooping in the attic, snooping in the basement, or snooping in the massive "carriage houses" (garages) in the backyard. I was happiest when left on my own to "get into" everything I could.

At the beginning of each day, our mother would dress us both, put us outside to play, and by the time I'd work my way around to the front of the house, I was filthy. She started putting me out the front door by the time I was three, just to show the neighbors that she really did try to keep me clean!

When not working at the restaurant, my grandmother's hobby was gardening, and while I frequently "raided" her vegetable garden, especially the berry patches, it was her rose garden that was famous. My grandmother's rose garden was not only enormous, it was pristine. I never picked or plucked anything in that flower garden. I knew even then that some things were meant to be left alone, but I did love to smell the flowers. I still love to stop and smell the flowers, but I am mostly disappointed in this endeavor today, because the hybrid versions of roses today have no fragrance at all. The roses back then, however, had 'flavors'!

In addition to the garden in the backyard, my grandmother also had a large, square, bathtub, sunk into the ground, on the south side of their house, which was her water-lily pond. On hot days during the summer, I could be found in the middle of this wonderfully mucky pond, fully dressed, smelling the water-lilies. They had 'flavor' too!

Throughout the summer and fall of 1951, I fed the squirrels that lived in the trees around "The Big House", and there was one particular squirrel that would literally climb into my lap and eat nuts from my hand. This squirrel had a baby in the spring of 1952, and she, and her baby, would come to me whenever I went outside, and would both eat from my hand. I have included a photograph of me feeding this squirrel in the photo library of this book. I loved feeding those squirrels.

One day, I was feeding the mommy squirrel, and Fred was feeding the baby. When the mommy was done eating, she hopped down

14

from my lap and was walking away, and Fred set the baby squirrel down. It wanted to eat more, so I picked up the baby squirrel and began to feed it. Quite by accident, the baby squirrel sank her sharp claws into my hand, and I accidentally dropped it to the ground. It screamed!

Mommy squirrel knew Fred had been feeding it, and she also knew I would never hurt her baby, so it must have been Fred who made the little squirrel scream. Making more noise than I had ever heard from any squirrel before, the mother squirrel bounded across the yard and attacked Fred, chasing his ass all around the house. Mom had to rescue him by chasing that mother squirrel off with a broom.

It was one of the funniest things I had ever seen, and I believe that it was during the course of this event that I learned to laugh from the depth of my heart. Until the day in Vietnam, when Larry Crotsley and I blew off the top of a mountain, this was the funniest single thing I had ever seen. I still laugh in the remembering, and the laugh still comes from the core of my being. It was hilarious!

Fred was running and screaming, the squirrel was chasing and chattering, and my poor mother was trying to separate the two. I laughed harder and louder than I had ever laughed before.

Shortly after this, in late May of 1952, my mother, who, as I said, contracted polio when she was nine years old, required extensive surgery to her right leg and hip. For months I was sent to live with my Aunt Louise (my "Other Mother"), and her husband, Uncle Ed.

One sunny summer day, dad and Fred, whom I had not seen for two months, came and took me for a ride. It was a great day. In spite of our differences, I even missed my brother. At any rate, we drove way out to the eastside, and driving down Liberty Boulevard, dad went to one of the little lakes in Liberty Park, where he rented a rowboat.

Just being together made this a very memorable day, but the memory was just beginning. When dad had rowed that boat to the middle of the lake, he pointed up toward a large building, which was Mount Sinai Hospital, and directed our attention to a sheet that was hanging from one of the upper floor rooms. There, in the window of that room, was our mom, waving to us from her hospital bed. I did not see my mother, father or brother again for another couple of months.

Later that year, just days before my fourth birthday, we were all back at The Big House, and Fred was given a set of drums for Christmas. If memory serves me correctly, there were three drums to the set, plus the cymbals. You know the kind I'm talking about. The drums were kept in the basement, and Fred would play down there for hours. That was great with me too, because as long as he was busy doing something else; he wasn't "beating me up".

One day that winter, however, I obviously did something to upset him, and he commenced to beat the crap out of me. At first break, I shot for the basement and, you guessed it, I kicked in every skin of his drum set. The noise was marvelous to my ears. Then I ran for my life! Needless to say, little Fred was one pissed-off dude.

At any rate, it was during these years that mom, dad, Fred and I would hop into the car, and drive way over to the Westside of Cleveland, where my mother's parents lived. Situ and Jiddu's house was a two-story, two-family residence, and living downstairs was my mom's brother, Raymond, my Aunt Mary, and their children. At this time, there was Kathy, who was just slightly younger than Fred, Barbara, who was three months younger than me, Loretta and Marlene. Linda and Raymond Jr. (better known as RayT) came later.

It was at this house though, I really had fun. First off, Situ didn't mind that I got dirty, and neither did anyone else.

The interesting thing about this house, however, was I remember living there before living in The Big House, but I never knew why we moved away. Aunt Lou explained it to me some years later, telling me that I lived here with Situ and Jiddu during my infancy, when my mother was in and out of the hospital. Between hospital trips, mom stayed here too, and her parents took care of her as she recovered from her surgeries (just as they had taken care of her

16

throughout her battle with polio). And Situ raised me while mom was hospitalized and recovering!

Fred and dad lived in The Big House on the Eastside, with grandma and grandpa during this time, and would visit on the weekends whenever mom was out of the hospital. Aunt Lou was surprised by how much I remembered from that time, but then, as I said, my memory solidly goes back to when I was two, when dad was in that accident.

Then, as I said earlier, in the spring of 1953, because dad could not drive delivery trucks any longer, mom and dad opened the F & L Delicatessen. Freddy-boy and I moved into the house behind the store early that summer, and we lived there for almost seven years.

(Thomas Jefferson)

"In matters of style, swim with the current;

In matters of principle, stand like a rock."

(Lawrence T. Vosen)

WINTERTIME

They say I'm in my wintertime,
and I should be at rest.
Some say I'm almost feeble,
and years past were my best!

They talk of by-passes and heart attacks,
and how I shouldn't push.
They say, "You've earned some good time off",
and I can turn to mush.

Yet from my core I truly know,
further from the truth they are.
For I have not arrived there yet,
although I've traveled far.

I never knew how to back down,
so why should I do so now,
After all, the fight's just beginning,
and through it I will plow.

Everything I have fought for,
everything I have believed;
is on the brink of toppling,
by those so ill-conceived.

All that's right and all that's good,
is under attack today.
So even if it's wintertime,
I'm in this fight to stay.

I'm here to fight for you and me,
And for my offspring too.
I'm here to fight for your self-worth,
and your inestimable value!

I'm here to fight for Freedom,
and for Ms. Liberty too.
I'm here to fight for me,
and I'm here to fight for you.

So join me in the battle folks,
whether springtime, summer or fall,
but really fall into the ranks,
you winter-timer's – One and All.

Chapter 2 – Childhood of Memories, Part II

The delicatessen was a complete change in lifestyle for all of us. Right from the start though, Fred and I began pitching in. I have frequently been asked, "Just what can a four-year-old do to help in a delicatessen?" I love answering that question.

The first thing the folks wanted to do was scrub the place; top to bottom. Dad worked along the shelving, removing everything off the top two or three shelves. I would be put onto a shelf with dry rags for dusting, then with the surface dust removed, a bucket of warm, soapy water was put on the shelf in front of me, and I would crawl on my hands and knees, scrubbing the shelves with a brush as I proceeded. Dad followed behind with drying towels. Meanwhile, Fred and mom were cleaning off the boxes or bottles of whatever belonged on the shelf. Once everything was clean, the product was put back, oldest in front. We learned how to clean and stock shelves early in life. That type of cleaning took place once every year, with regular dusting all the time. The place was immaculate, which was the only way F & L would allow it.

Another task, repeated weekly, involved cleaning the meat cabinets, and although the glass and outer surfaces were wiped down daily, everything was taken apart and given a thorough scouring on a weekly basis. Here again, this time with a hose hooked-up to the hot water heater, little Larry would crawl into the bottom of the meat display cases, and scour them out. Seeing as I did not care about getting dirty, I actually enjoyed these chores. I was contributing, and that was important to me.

Before I turned five, I began waking at 4:00 A.M. on Saturday mornings, so I could go with my dad to shop for the store. Together we would go to the Eastside Market, the Farmers Market, the Central Market, the Westside Market, and then the Fish monger at the foot of W.25th Street. Almost from the start, once we got to Train Avenue, dad would put me on his lap and let me steer the car as we drove this winding street. "Driving" Train Avenue was always the most exciting part of the day. When Fred came, we always alternated the driving. We both learned early.

I loved being with my dad, and our time together on Saturdays was the best. Even though he spent most of the day talking with his friends, ruining me for life in regard to shopping, I was still able to spend serious time with him, and I reveled in being at his side! Personally, I do not recall Fred coming with us too often on those Saturday treks, but like me, Fred did not like waiting for dad to stop talking with people. We used to have to beg dad to keep moving, or else we'd never get done... So, I think Fred frequently opted to stay at home, especially as we grew older and he was better able to help mom in the deli, while dad and I did the shopping.

I can't continue without telling you that our dad was an amazing guy! Dad's gift; his coin (besides his loving and compassionate heart), manifested itself significantly through his ability to remember people's names and faces, and the names of their spouses, their children, and any significant events that might have taken place in their family. His memory, coupled to the fact that he really did care about people, caused our dad to be truly loved. And, it didn't seem to matter where we went, or where we traveled, dad always seemed to know someone. Always!

I have dozens of memories of being with him when suddenly we'd hear, "Hey, Fred, how are you? How's Laurice?" And in turning to the voice, dad would always recognize the person, and would commence to ask about their wife/husband, kids (by name), any grandchildren, and would always have the capacity to ask something like, "How did Barbara's surgery turn out?" or, "How did that test turn out?" or, "Did you get that job?" And in many instances, the event he was inquiring about had happened two or three or five years earlier. Without exaggeration, our dad was phenomenal in this regard; he consistently used his coin to brighten someone's day!

I am told that I have inherited some of his compassion and empathy, but this other gift: remembering names, faces, and events – sadly, has eluded me completely. In this, he was truly blessed.

At any rate, by the time I was five, I was also doing dishes nightly, and the first dishwashing lesson I learned was, "You can't cut grease with cold water!" Eventually, I was able to withstand water straight from the hot water tank, and that was turned to high!

In the summer of 1954, Fred and I were sent to alert our upstairs neighbors that a "Tornado Warning" had been issued; prompting them to head for the basement. I did not know what a tornado was, only that we all needed to head underground. On our way to the basement though, as soon as Fred and I entered the house, we heard what sounded like a massive freight train in our backyard. Turning to see what was making the noise, we watched as a huge twister danced before our eyes. The space between our garage and the door we were standing behind was no more than fifty feet, yet that twister played between the two structures just for us, for what seemed an eternity. Thankfully, our heavenly Father moved that tornado away from the house, leveling a neighbor's garage instead, while lifting a huge tree out of the ground and throwing it over an alley and four yards. We played on that fallen tree for weeks before city workers finally removed it.

By the time I was six years old, I was carrying cases of soda and beer up from the basement into the walk-in cooler. Other dry goods were hauled up as well. By the time I was eight, I was easily toting the 50 pound sacks of potatoes and onions down and up those eighteen stairs. Needless to say, Freddy-boy and I were both building muscles in those early years.

Then, in the spring of 1955, dad somehow acquired a gaggle of geese and a flock of ducks. We made a pen using the house storm windows for an enclosure, and Fred and I were responsible for feeding and watering our "farm animals". I had never seen critters being born, so that summer was intriguing, to say the least. They had a lot of babies. As the gaggle and flock grew, our enclosure required expanding, and our repeated requests for more storm windows, and the increased noise emanating from the backyard, finally wore-out dad's patience.

Grabbing a stack of empty boxes, dad walked into the pen and started stuffing the ducks and geese into those boxes, which he then loaded into the back of our delivery van. Loading Fred and me into the van as well, dad drove to a building I had never visited before. He backed the van to the delivery bay dock, and started tossing the boxes loaded with our geese and ducks onto the dock. A couple of dock-workers put the boxes on a conveyor, and we watched as our critters disappeared on that conveyor through a hole in the ceiling.

As usual, dad visited with the workers, while Fred and I stood / sat waiting for him to leave. But, we didn't go anywhere for some time. Then, all of a sudden, boxes full of wrapped packages began coming down another conveyor from that upstairs area, and dad loaded those boxes into the van, and we went home.

Using "whitewash" on the front window of the store, dad wrote a "Special Sale" sign advertising: "FRESH DUCK AND GEESE FOR SALE" and that was the end of our days as ranchers. I don't know if the word, "traumatized" fits here, but when mom served a roasted goose for dinner the night after the slaughter, I don't recall being able to eat very much, and although I have enjoyed eating roasted duck over the years, I still don't recall ever eating goose. (Snakes and rodents and monkeys and all sort of other critters while in Vietnam, yes, but goose? I don't think so).

Late in the summer of 1955, Mom, Dad, Fred and I stood in line at Lakewood High School, where the Jonas Salk polio vaccine was being administered. Three times we stood in line to receive the vaccine that would prevent us from catching the disease that ravaged mom at such a young age. Having contracted polio did not make her immune to the disease either, so mom took the sugar cubes, containing the vaccine, right along with us. And each trip would elicit tears of joy from her, knowing that her kids, and every other kid, would never again suffer as did she!

The spring and summer of 1957, was an extremely eventful period, to say the least. I was eight years old:

First, Freddy-boy and I asked if we could build a "soap-box racer" from scrap wood that was out in the garage. "Not without supervision, and I don't have time right now", was the reply. We went out to the garage and began building the thing anyway!

22

Dad had two hammers in his toolbox, so we were in great shape. The first hammer was a typical 'claw' type, but the second was actually a hunting hatchet with a hammer-head on the other end. Fred, being the eldest, insisted that he have the claw hammer, leaving me with the hatchet thing.

Work progressed nicely on our racer, but somehow, Fred ended up behind me, working on something, while I was hammering away at something else. Suddenly, in the middle of a backswing with my hammer, I felt some resistance, and turning to see what was in my way, I saw where I had planted the hatchet squarely on top of Fred's head, and blood was literally gushing down his face from the gash.

Screaming, I ran for the house. I knew we were going to need help. As I ran toward the side entrance though, I was suddenly hit by something from behind, which sent me sprawling to the ground in agony. In retaliation for splitting his head open, even with his vision blurred because of the blood, Fred caught me in the middle of my back with his claw hammer, at about twenty-five feet. Not a bad toss, all things considered.

You can only imagine the look on dad's face when he came running out of the store, only to see Son #1 bleeding like a stuck pig, and Son #2 lying on the ground writhing in pain. We were both rushed to the hospital!

About a month later, in preparation for my First Communion, dad and I, along with Fred and one of my brothers' friends, Jack, were making the rounds, picking up things here, and ordering stuff there. The ultimate goal was to stop by the tailor who was getting my suit ready. At one of our stops, I saw one of my friends riding his bike, and he stopped to chat. I was sitting "shot-gun" while Fred and Jack were in the back. At any rate, my friend had a really neat stopwatch, and somehow I swapped something I had with me for that stopwatch. (I still have that watch today!) Dad finally finished whatever it was he was doing, and off we went, heading toward downtown Cleveland, and the tailor, via Train Avenue.

As he drove, I was telling dad about the stopwatch, and he asked to see it. Well, good old Fred and Jack had been looking at it, and had dropped it on the floor. Somehow, it ended up under the passenger side of the front seat. When I asked for the watch, I was told to get it myself, so – turning around in the seat, and reaching way over the back of the front seat, I reached to get the stopwatch on the floor. As I reached, my foot caught on the door handle just as dad was taking a left curve on the winding road, and in an instant, the door flew open, and out I went!

I landed headfirst (face first, actually) in the gravel parking lot of a trucking company, stopping about three feet short of smashing into a telephone pole. I recall standing, with my hands over my face, as I watched dad stop the car, leap out, and run toward me. When I moved my hands from my face, and saw them covered with blood, I lost it! Dad ripped off his shirt, covered my bloody face, and off we raced to the hospital for the second time that spring.

Surprisingly, there were no actual cuts anywhere on my face or body, just scrapes and scratches. While I did develop some ugly scabs for a short time, they eventually disappeared and all was well.

Some months later, on the 4th of July, the whole family was able to go to Edgewater Beach on the Westside of Cleveland, to watch the fireworks display. We stayed way later than the display though, relaxing and cooking hot dogs and marshmallows over a great fire. Dad, as always, had a wonderful assortment of firecrackers, cherry bombs and stuff, and every once in a while he or one of my uncles would set some off.

As the night wore on, I recall all of us lounging on the warm sand around the fire, when two policemen stopped by to see how we were doing, and warned us against setting off any illegal fireworks. My mother told them that all was well, and that actually, we were packing up for home. In her effort to clean up our mess though, my dear mother grabbed some bags and threw them into the fire, thinking it was all garbage leftover from our snacks. One of those bags, however, contained all the remaining fireworks that the folks had, and within moments, with the police about fifty yards away, all hell broke loose as firecrackers, cherry bombs and hammerheads began exploding. Red rockets were glaring too!

Naturally, we kids laughed until our sides hurt, but I thought mom was going to die. The policemen simply turned around, looked at us as we laughed, saw mom's frightened look, and joined us in laughter as they turned and walked away. I don't recall ever seeing my mother as embarrassed as she was that day.

The following summer, which ended-up being our last full summer at the store, had two unusual events. Both are impossible to forget:

First, during our years at the store, dad never took a vacation. This summer though, things turned out a bit different. Our Uncle John, Aunt Loretta, and cousins, Bill, Bob and Bud had returned from Morocco, where Major Shalala had been stationed. Uncle John was being transferred to somewhere in the United States, so while he was settling in, Aunt Loretta was available to help mom in the store. Bud was deemed too young to go on this particular trip, so he stayed with the ladies and helped too, but dad was taking the rest of the guys on a vacation.

My parents had an Austin-Healey Model A-40 van that they used for making deliveries, but the van was now to be used as our mode of transportation on a camping trip. We were heading to East Harbor State Park in Lakeside, Ohio, about 85 miles from Cleveland. For me, it was a million miles from the inner-city, and it couldn't have been more perfect.

Working with a shoe-string budget, dad meticulously packed the van with everything imaginably needed for this camping trip, which was to last a week. A week! We didn't have a tent, so dad borrowed a very large piece of canvas, and a very thick rope. Draping the canvas over the rope, which was tied to two trees, dad made a really large impromptu tent, and that was the sleeping quarters for most of the guys. Dad and I slept in the van.

My first-cousins: Jerry, Bill, Bob and Jim were going, along with Fred and me. And if that weren't enough, two of the guys from the neighborhood were invited: Billie and the aforementioned Jack. Nine guys altogether, including dad.

The van was packed from side-to-side, and almost from the floor to the ceiling. Dad drove, I sat on a coke box between the two front seats, Jerry sat shotgun, and the rest of the guys sort of sprawled out atop all of the stuff that was packed into the van. The drive from Cleveland to Lakeside today, takes about 90 minutes, thanks to the Interstate system. Back in the day though, the Interstate didn't exist, and the drive was a three hour riot. We had more fun bouncing around in that van than could possibly be described.

Once we arrived at the park, found our camping site, set-up the "tent", and unloaded the van, we all set-off for another spot in the park, where dad rented a rowboat for the week. Six of the guys jumped into the boat, as the rest of us drove back to the campsite. We waited – and waited – and waited – for the six to row their way to the designated spot.

The more time that passed, the more frantic dad became! He worried about the fate of the guys. Standing on the shore of Lake Erie, calling to where he thought they might be, we finally heard voices calling back in the dark – asking for help! The dummies broke one of the oars, and were stuck somewhere out on Lake Erie. Dad was able to get help from some nice guy who had a power boat, and they towed the rowboat to shore. By the time we finally got settled in for the night, everyone was exhausted, and sleep came fast. We got a replacement oar the following morning.

For the next week we played, fished for perch and walleye, swam, ate like pigs, and had an absolute ball. Having so much fun himself, dad phoned home and asked if we could stay another few days – and, "You better wire some more money!" (There were no such things as credit or debit cards back then folks, so Western Union was the only way to get cash from one place to another).

After the additional funds arrived, we had to do some shopping, so we all jumped into the van and off we headed for the grocery store. On the way to the store, dad saw a wild rabbit out in a field, and the chase was on! Cousin Jerry jumped out of the van, stood on the passenger side running board, and holding onto the van door with his left hand, he tried to kill that rabbit with that hatchet/hammer in his right hand, as dad maneuvered the van in an ongoing chase. Everyone else simply held on for dear life as that rabbit ran for his! The rabbit escaped, but we laughed so hard, and had so much fun, we really didn't care about that poor bunny.

In hindsight, as I consider the trip in its entirety, I realize that our escapades, including riding in the van the way we did, would probably cost dad a few thousand dollars in fines TODAY. There were no seatbelts back then though. There were no rules about riding in the back of pickup trucks or vans either. Half the stuff we did would not even be possible today, because laws have changed, or because places are considerably more overcrowded then when these events took place. But oh my goodness, did we ever have fun. East Harbor State Park!

The second memorable thing that summer occurred a few weeks after we got home from vacation.

As I've said before, our mother contracted polio when she was nine years old. The disease severely impacted her right leg and hip. Over the course of her life, she spent months upon months in hospitals, and years in bed. Walking from the house to the car, especially in the wintertime, always required an escort or two for her to lean on. One day, mom told us she wanted to go for a walk. It was a beautiful late summer day, and the warmth of the day, and the bright shining sun was more than she could take.

Before contracting polio, my mother was a tomboy (we were told). There were times, as Fred and I were growing, when she'd come outside and play catch with us. Our aim had to be good, because she couldn't maneuver well, so one of us always played back-up behind her. Nevertheless, the lady knew how to play ball! She knew a lot about a lot of stuff, and she loved watching us play as well.

Anyway, on this particular day, she wanted to go for a walk, so Fred and I escorted her. We thought we'd head west on Storer Avenue, to the corner, and then turn back. When we got to the

27

corner though, she wanted to keep going, so we headed north. She actually wanted to walk around the block! It was a good thing we started our walk early though, because when the neighbors (who were all customers at the store) saw her out, they naturally invited her (us) in for a visit. We ultimately stopped to visit at least six or seven of our neighbors. The walk around the block lasted for hours, but what a day it was. I had never seen my mother so happy or carefree.

[After contracting polio, bed-ridden 24/7, mom had tutors for her schooling. In order to break the monotony, my grandparents also hired a music teacher, who taught her to read music and play the harmonica. Now it may not be a big deal to many people that our mom could play a harmonica, but as anyone from my family and I would testify, that lady could play the harmonica with the best professionals anywhere, anytime. She was amazing!

I recall being told, that when the Hohner manufacturer of harmonicas came out with the "Chromonica" model harmonica (which is the twenty-four reed model with a "slide" for hitting 'flat' notes, and which was only available in Europe at the time), mom's music teacher wrote to the company in Germany, asking if they would sell one of the new models to mom. The folks at Hohner sent her one, free!

And with that harmonica, our mother could play any song. Adding to her abilities though, is the fact that she could play any song by ear, having heard that song only one time.]

I am mentioning the harmonica here, because something special happened that day as we walked around the block, and I've never forgotten the beauty of the event.

We were on the southward leg of our walk around the block, a bit more than 75% complete, when the last of the neighbor ladies invited us in to visit. Clearly, it was a good thing too, because Fred and I could tell that mom was getting tired. As we entered the living room of the house, we could not help but notice the beautiful piano sitting off to the side of the room. It was gorgeous.

The lady provided lemonade for us all, and as we sat, the ladies began to chat about this and that. Suddenly, mom began asking about the piano. Then, mom boldly asked if she could try and play the instrument. Our mother did not know how to play the piano, nor had she ever had an opportunity to actually sit at a piano. Nevertheless, she wanted to see if she could "figure it out". The lady very graciously gave permission, and mom moved over to the gorgeous instrument. She plucked at the keys for a few moments, like any of us would. Then with her right hand, she began playing a very simple song – one finger, one key. It was cute!

Once she "figured it out" though, putting both hands on the keyboard, my mother started playing a couple of songs. Without sheet music, mind you, she played that piano as if she had been playing the instrument for years. And as she played, tears slowly streamed down her cheeks. After playing her favorite song, "Greenfields", mom turned away from the piano, dried the tears from her cheeks and thanked the lady for allowing her to do something that she had always wanted to do, which was to try and play a piano! Needless to say, we were stunned!

It wasn't long after that we were back on our trek, heading for home, having received an invite from the lady to "please come back and play again if you ever feel up to it". Sadly, mom never took another walk like that again, and I never saw her play the piano again. But for that one day, I watched and listened; spellbound, as my mom really displayed her musical talent.

When we finally got home, mom was exhausted, and immediately went to bed. I think it took three days for her to fully recover from the strenuous walk, but I remember hearing her tell dad about it all, and she cried again when she talked about finally being able to play the piano!

[Years later, after our parents died, Fred and I each ended with one of mom's harmonicas. Although I cannot read music at all, in spite of a friend trying to teach me, I sort of began playing that harmonica, figuring out the notes as I went along. I cannot play by ear, but if I know a song, I can make my own kind of "sheet music", and from those personal notes I can belt out a fairly nice rendition of a number of songs (mostly faith-based, but some contemporary too). I don't play much anymore, but during the height of my "practicing", I also sat at a piano one day, and with one hand, one finger, I was able to play a song I knew, and I had tears in my eyes as I recalled the day that mom seriously "played the piano". Isn't it amazing how memories can flood our hearts and overwhelm us at times?]

There is one more note regarding our mother that should be mentioned, because this small thing impacted me for years. (I do not know how it affected Fred, but I'm certain it did in some way):

During her recovery from polio, Situ and Jiddu thought it would be nice for her to have a pet, so they got her a cat to play with. As it turned out, that was a bad idea, because for whatever reason, the cat bit her. She was deathly afraid of cats for the remainder of her life. Therefore, before she would go outside from anywhere, Fred and I were sent out on "cat patrol", to chase away any cat we saw. After we returned, and reported the area "cat free", mom would come outside. Naturally, I grew up hating cats!

When I was stationed in Germany, one of the men I was stationed with lived off-base with his wife. Roger and Verna, who I called "mom and pops", sort of adopted me, and had me over to their apartment frequently. Roger and Verna had the biggest damned cat I had ever seen. My initial reaction to the cat, as you might imagine, was not favorable, but he was a friendly cat. I never knew cats could be friendly! After their monster cat leapt onto the back of the couch and wrapped itself around my neck a few times, purring as I'd finally begin petting it, I got over my cat phobia. I never told mom, but once I was discharged from the Army, I'd go on her cat patrols with a totally different attitude.

Chapter 3 – Childhood of Memories, Part III

We moved away from the delicatessen when I was ten, and our lives changed radically once again. Although dad continued finding part-time work on Saturday's, and even though I continued going with him on those Saturday work days, we all had a lot more time to do family things.

On the weekends, during the wintertime especially, once Fred and I were done practicing or playing a game in whichever sport was in season, we would rush home and play cards with/against mom and dad. Many times the Aunts and Uncles would come to the house as well, and various card games would be played in these family gatherings.

Further adding to the family times though, were the picnics. Arrangements for the family picnics would be made weeks in advance, because our picnics were epic. Although we had a number of places where we could go, our favorite spot was Tamsin Lake Park, a private park in Peninsula, Ohio, southeast of Cleveland. We would try to have at least two or three of these picnics every summer.

There was always a race to see which family could arrive at the park earliest, and we won this race more often than not. Arriving early, Fred and I would pull together any number of picnic tables, because we knew that forty to sixty people would be attending. As we arranged the tables, mom and dad would begin cooking breakfast.

Uncle Ray, Aunt Mary and my six cousins normally arrived afterward, and cooking was done to feed that group as well. Other cousins, aunts and uncles would arrive throughout the morning, and our grandparents would get there last, normally by lunchtime. Cooking was an ongoing operation. And we would play and swim all day!

Cleveland weather, however, inevitably would bring a rainstorm of some degree during the day, and this is when the real fun began. Mom would unpack her harmonica, we guys would unpack our Lebanese hand held (or lap held) drums, and rushing for a pavilion, we'd all begin playing Lebanese music. The ladies would be dancing, and everyone in the park would rush for shelter, and watch as my family played, laughed and danced. And this happened all the time!

The best part of it all though, was when we'd get strangers to join in on the dancing. While mom played the harmonica, and the guys played the drums, my aunts and cousins would pull strangers into the 'dancing circle' and teach them how to dance Lebanese style. It was a riot. And not surprising, the music and dancing would normally continue for a considerable time after the rain stopped.

We gathered frequently as a family, and it did not require a holiday.

Some years after my mother died, I was sitting with Aunt Lou talking about times past, and my Aunt revealed something I never knew or understood. The family all assumed that Aunt Lou was the "Matriarch" of mom's side of the family, and in many ways she was. But, it was my mother who was the instigator of ALL the gatherings. It was my mom who'd make the calls, set-up the reservations, and make things happen.

In putting all these things together, I realize I inherited many of my relationship skills from my dad, but from my mother I inherited this thing for family and unity, and it wasn't until well after they were both gone before I realized the fullness of it all.

Every winter, especially while we were at the store, our mother would contract pneumonia, or double-pneumonia. She was advised to move to Arizona for her health decades before she died, at age 50, but there was no way our mother was ever leaving her family.

The pneumonia issue, by the way, only added to some already outrageous medical bills, which along with everything else simply added more pressure to an already tight budget. Strange and wondrous things happened though, which would satisfy some financial need or another, and of these things I must make note: One year, I remember mom winning 2nd prize in the church raffle. It was either a trip to Florida for four, or $2,000.00. They needed almost that amount to get out of a financial hole, so they opted for the cash. Then we went out for Chinese food!

We always went to a special Chinese restaurant on Madison Avenue whenever a bill got paid off, or, whenever extra money miraculously showed up. On the miraculous side, let me provide an example:

One day, this guy came to the store and talked to my dad as if they'd known each other for years. I have already told you about my dad's memory in regard to people, and to the day he died, dad swore that he had never met this guy before in his life. At any rate, this guy came into the store, and told dad that he was on his way to Florida's Hialeah Park – Race Horse Track, and he had a tip on a horse. He asked dad for $20.00 and told him that he'd return "after the season" with his winnings.

My parents didn't have money to spare, but whenever they saw someone in need, they would dig deep and help the person as best they could. In this instance, dad actually gave the man $20.00, never thinking he'd see him again. Months passed before this same man came to the store, and gave my father an envelope containing over $800.00. Bills were paid, and we ate Chinese!

The same guy showed up two years later, gave dad the same story, and again dad gave him $20.00. And again, some months later, the guy gave dad an envelope containing more than $600.00. Bills were paid, and we ate Chinese!

In each of these situations, my parents were in a pinch for some hundreds of dollars, and out of nowhere this guy showed-up with every penny they needed, plus enough for a Chinese dinner. Such were the miracles that happened throughout my lifetime, with regard to my parents and finances. And I guess this is where I need to talk about my poker winnings from Vietnam, because it all fits so naturally.

I have no doubt you will question what I am going to reveal regarding my savings account, once you read the events that drove me to enlist in the Army in 1966. I will provide an explanation momentarily though, which I pray will put the puzzle pieces together for you, because when I returned home from Vietnam in 1968, I had exactly $235.00 in that savings account...

Three weeks after I left for Vietnam, my dad injured his back. Sadly, the injury was not work related, so there was no workers comp. Out of work, with no insurance, and no means of income, the checks I sent home every month, both my paychecks and the additional poker winnings, all went to pay the mortgage, buy food and clothing, and pay off the doctor bills, both for him and mom. Generally, the money was used to take care of my folks.

Before leaving Nha Trang, Vietnam, on my way home, I sent a certified check to myself in Cleveland for a bit over $6,000.00. This was my poker fund, hidden in the legs of my cot at Dak-Pek. In addition to this money, I also received my mustering-out pay in Fort Lewis, Washington. That sum equaled a bit more than $3,000.00. So, when I got home from Vietnam, I had a bit over $9,000.00 to my name.

When my dad came home on November 21, 1968, later in the day after my arrival, it was not because he was coming home from work. He was coming from the Union Hall where he had waited all day, hoping for a delivery driver job for that day. The next day, when I thought he was taking a day off to take me around town to visit our old friends, he was taking a day off from looking for work at the Hall.

Dad did find another permanent job about two weeks after I came home, and to the best of my knowledge he never hit the unemployment line again. But, for seventeen months, my pay, and the very prolific poker winnings that came to me, was a miraculous gift needed to sustain my family.

I cannot say I wasn't disappointed, nor can I say I was not upset when I learned the truth of these things, because, to a large degree, I was very upset. I was extremely disappointed that they didn't tell

34

me; that they didn't confide in me; that they kept this all a secret from me! That was my disappointment!

In a recent conversation with a family member, I was told, "Much of what was happening back home was held back in the letters to you." No one wanted to worry me. The family was more concerned for my safety. Two times I was almost sent for, to take an emergency leave, but my mother would not allow it. She had read that many men returning to Vietnam from emergency leave, were not returned to their original units, and she feared I would be given an even more dangerous assignment.

Because of the continuous miracles that I had witnessed in regard to money throughout my childhood, I learned very early-on that money is never an issue! I have tried to teach this lesson to others, but it is a difficult lesson to learn. The fullness of the matter, however, is that *IF* my Father in Heaven wants me to have a million dollars this instant – a million dollars will be available to me. (Peter took money from the mouth of a fish to pay taxes for him and the Messiah). Money is NEVER the issue. In this regard, money is like fear: It's what you do with it that matters!

I believe that many people are given a great deal of money as a test. Sadly, many, many people fail that test. On the other hand, if you are a disciplined disciple in NEED of a great deal of money, in order to accomplish a particular task, the needed money will always be made available.

I was tremendously "lucky" at poker in Vietnam, because a huge need existed at home, which required I win at poker. And, I have never been as 'lucky' since. Today, it is clear that the need does not exist as it did back then. I still play to win, always, but that 'luck' thing just isn't there anymore.

Nevertheless, I can honestly say that throughout my life, every true NEED I have ever had has been met. Even during the three, three-year periods of unemployment I incurred throughout the course of my career – our needs were always met. Always! And I am always amazed when I recollect these things. The sum that was sent home, by the way, exceeded $50,000.00.

35

I never saw any of it!

I never knew how to back down, so I plowed through…

(Abraham Lincoln)

"I am not bound to win, but I am bound to be true. I am not bound to succeed, but I am bound to live by the light that I have. I must stand with anybody that stands right, and stand with him while he is right, and part with him when he goes wrong."

Chapter 4 – My Tumultuous Years, Part I

For the longest time, I thought I would begin this book by telling many more of the wonderful stories and memories I have of my childhood, and from that base, transition into the stage that I personally refer to as, "My Tumultuous Years". My thinking was that I could gradually show how despair entered into a life of joy. The more I thought of these things though, the more I realized that the very core of this book emanates from the lessons I learned in the near three year period immediately preceding my entry into the Army. Enough memories have been provided though, for you to recognize the stark contrast between these two periods of my life. Personally, the transition between my youth and my tumultuous years was like walking into and through a very thick brick wall, and the value and significance of the lessons I learned were equally difficult to acquire.

Therefore, I am going to stop injecting stories of my childhood for a while, and focus on the most difficult story I have ever told. This is difficult, only because reliving the events is hard. Some things are best left alone, but I hope what I am about to share with you, may somehow be useful to you.

After "A Diamond on The Wall" was published, I awoke one morning to thoughts racing through my mind regarding the three years preceding my enlistment into the Army, and how those events impelled, propelled and compelled me to make the decisions I did. I awoke to memories of fights, and rumbles, and arguments, and battles, external and internal. As I pondered these matters, it occurred to me that some young boy or girl, somewhere, might "see themselves" in what I lived, and realize that they are not a freak, a retard, an outcast, a nerd, unloved or unlovable. And in the seeing of this truth, they might find hope!

As I consider those three years, however, and compare my memories with the things I see and hear today, I realize that nothing has changed. Nothing is different. Nothing is new. Things and people are as evil or good today as they were then. The difference between 21st Century society, and the culture of the 1950's and early 1960's, is that world population has almost tripled in the past sixty years, and the manner and speed in which we receive and absorb our news has transformed dramatically.

Additionally, much of the news and publicity of our day is intentionally manipulated and biased, which makes what we see and hear, suspect, counterproductive, frequently demoralizing, and destructive. I believe these manipulations are intentionally designed to diminish our willingness to engage; designed to diminish our value; designed to fulfill the agendas of a very select, self-serving, vocal minority.

While I will never waver in my conviction regarding my heavenly Father's hand guiding me through every moment of my life, it was during the two and one-half years I spent in high school, that I felt furthest from any form of "Godly love".

By the first day of what would have been my sophomore year, I was convinced I had four friends. Had it not been for those three young men, and one lovely young lady, I cannot begin to imagine where life would have taken me. This is why I do not question or judge friendships or associations amongst people today. This is why I advise parents against making rash judgments about their children's friends. (Monitor, yes! Dictate and manipulate, no!) It is a cliché, but unless we walk in a person's shoes, and experience the things they are experiencing, we do not know why any person acts as they do. Therefore, we do not have the right to make assumptions in regard to their actions, motives, or relationships.

Without an unbiased investigation of events in a person's life, and without candid, non-judgmental conversation, "Talking" becomes lecturing, "Teaching" becomes scolding and "Inquiry" becomes inquisition. And from that point, all levels of communication simply evaporate into a mist of futility. I experienced this first-hand back then, because matters evolved to the point where relations with my family elders simply fell apart. I am experiencing this same thing today at a totally different level. Nothing is new!

Although I did have one particular fulfilling relationship with a mature individual, even that relationship developed too late to make a difference. By the time I was seventeen, things were well underway, and there was no turning back.

The events revealed in the following two chapters have been exposed to only three people throughout my life, and in each telling, I expressed a knowing that my four "ruffians" were placed in my life for my well-being. I acknowledged my Father's intervention in their placement and involvement. To this end, I have always prayed He would reward them for the role they played, for without them, I might have surrendered all hope; a wholly uncharacteristic trait for me!

Further, as I pondered the thoughts racing through my mind that morning, it also occurred to me that some middle-aged or elderly members of our society might recall the tumultuous years of their youth, and in their recollections, garner the strength to once again fight the fight. In our silence, many within the next generations think we do not know or understand the battles they are fighting. Feeling alone, they are surrendering. They need our help; and they need it now!

I found peace as I realized that in this telling, I might be reaching out to a younger generation, who seem to be racing hopelessly off a cliff, out of control, while also reaching out to an older generation who believe that all control has been lost. Both positions are horribly wrong.

The truth lies in the fact that everything is under the complete control of our Heavenly Father.

I know, "That's religious". "That is not something we talk about in public".

Oh, how wrong our thinking is if we believe that nonsense!

Society is "out of control" today because we have in fact turned our back on the One who created us. We are ignoring the simplicity of

39

the life HE wishes us to have and live. **But that is not the approach I am going to take.** I am not going to use a religious or spiritual approach to present these matters to you. So please, allow me to reveal what I learned as a teenager and young adult. I promise to not get spiritually over-zealous.

(Thomas Jefferson)

"And the day will come, when the mystical generation of Jesus, by the Supreme Being as His Father, in the womb of a virgin, will be classed with the fable of the generation of Minerva, in the brain of Jupiter."

Chapter 5 – My Tumultuous Years, Part II

I graduated from St. Boniface Elementary School, a Catholic grade school on the Westside of Cleveland, Ohio, in 1963. I attended classes at this highly academic school for a full eight years. As I type these words, I am literally looking at a photograph of my graduation class, and in the looking, I remember. I remember it all so very clearly. I remember them too, my friends and classmates. Many of us were so "tight" in our relationships back then that just the thought of not being with each other anymore was overwhelming. Many were so deeply saddened by that thought, they literally wept!

Friendships aside, it took eight years to work our way up the ladder within the "society" of that elementary school, and we relished being at 'the top of the heap'. For me personally, not having to follow in the footsteps of a "perfect" brother, made the final two years in this setting even more gratifying and enjoyable. My brother had moved on to high school, and for a brief period, I was my own man!

And please understand that Fred, personally, did nothing wrong. He was who he was, and anyone trying to compare us would automatically recognize huge differences. Fred and I had the same last name, and we came from the same nurturing home, but we were nothing alike, and anyone trying to compare us, or anyone trying to compare any two people, is simply showing their ignorance. I was a bit more of a handful than Fred. I had a sharp wit, and I enjoyed joking, but a lot of the teachers did not like that. I also had a lot to offer too, but I resented their moronic, "You're nothing like your brother", comparisons, so I went into a hole.

With all this in mind, imagine how it felt, being a high school freshman – walking into the largest High School in the city of Cleveland. The comparisons with Fred began immediately. And, I was alone. A few of my elementary school classmates were also freshmen at West Tech, but in the maze of 5,000 students, 1,200 of which were freshmen, locating my friends was impossible.

From day one, things began "shaking-out" in the freshman class. This is no different today than it was back then. We had jocks, nerds, and almost every other sub-class kids sort themselves into. And, each group had to find their leaders and followers. The selection process was sometimes simple, or sometimes complex.

Personally, I was a jock! At least I thought I was a jock. I had started playing football, baseball and basketball in the 2nd grade, and I was pretty good at all three. Football was my primary sport, then baseball. I loved to play, and I loved to win! I began playing for West Tech's freshman team in the summer of 1963, and had won a starting position as the team's half-back.

In addition to thinking I was a jock though, I also knew I was not a dummy. The elementary school education I had received for eight years was solid, so I also wanted to establish myself in my new school as academically accomplished. I wanted to learn how to debate. I wanted to take difficult college-prep classes. I wanted to be athletically and academically challenged. And, I wanted to be successful in ALL of these endeavors.

But here's the thing: It didn't matter what we thought we were, or what our intentions were. It boiled down to how we were perceived by others in those first days. What made things difficult for me, was I was a physical freak.

At the beginning of the ninth grade, I had a 44" chest, a 20" neck, arms like a gorilla, legs of iron, and a 28" inch waist. All of that was packed into a 4'10" tall, 150 pound body. In spite of being on the football team, or maybe even because I was on the team, my appearance brought all sorts of issues.

My physical attributes literally frightened some of the kids, because I "looked tough". Whether I behaved in a threatening manner or not was irrelevant. Appearance was everything, just as it is today, because kids love to judge a book by its cover. In the sight of many, I was a threat because of that initial impression. Much to my dismay, most of the nice kids avoided me.

I need for you to understand that I never started a fight with another student. NEVER! I never backed-down either, but that's another subject altogether, isn't it?! I never bullied, taunted, or challenged anyone. PERIOD! I defended myself, and I even helped defend others, but I never initiated, and that is vital to the credibility of this book.

Nevertheless, my status within the class was challenged between fourth and fifth period on the first day of my freshman year. One of the other freshman boys decided to attack me, from behind, shoving me and my books to a hallway floor. With all the strength I could muster, I leapt from the floor and threw one punch – smack in the middle of the smirking offender's face. I knocked-out my attacker with one punch, picked up my books, and continued to my next class. Needless to say, I was stunned and confused by the encounter, because I didn't recall ever seeing this kid before!

The following day, this same young man blocked my path as I tried to enter a classroom. Sporting two black eyes and a broken nose, I asked if he really wanted a repeat of the previous day's events. He declined, deferring to his much larger friend, who I happened to see reflected in the glass of the door (behind me). As he began moving to attack me, I instinctively held the classroom door, bent forward at the waist, raised my right leg behind me, and with all the strength I could muster, I kicked backward into the mid-section of my attacker. Once he was doubled over, I spun, thrust my palm downward once in the back of his head, and knocked him to the floor. Turning back to the classroom doorway, I pushed my way past my day one attacker, attended class, and wondered just how long this stupidity was going to continue.

I was horribly saddened. In spite of what I had hoped to accomplish academically and athletically, the events of the first two days were repeated over and over. Every day was a challenge, and every day was a new battle. One teacher witnessed the attack on day one, and two teachers saw the event on day two. None of the three said or reported anything. More disheartening, none came to my aid or defense either, as is often the case today. I was suspended two days for these fights!

[There are kids in schools today who, while they may not be challenged physically to defend themselves, are nonetheless fighting for their very existence. Fighting for the right to simply live and learn. While they struggle to exist, others belittle, tease or bully them. Today, the taunting occurs in person and electronically, making them feel even more inferior in many ways. All the while, teachers, administrators and parents remain oblivious or uncaring to their plight.]

And it was the same back in the 1960's. Nothing is new!

In my case, matters grew worse daily. Within four weeks I had defeated some twenty different boys who wanted to unseat the individual perceived to be the top "hood" of the class. A number of these fights brought about one and two day suspensions and these suspensions caused me to lose my position on the football team. All hope of being with the jocks, or accomplishing stellar levels of academic achievement flew out the window. I was in a battle for my very existence, and everything else fell to the wayside.

Beginning my fifth week, I was leaving the school, and was jumped by three young men, whom I had already defeated. In a matter of moments two of my attackers were on the ground; the third was heading home. The next day, there were four! Sadly, during all these events, all I wanted was to be left alone, and no one understood that.

Fortunately for me, when the four guys jumped me, a sophomore, who I later learned was nick-named, "Pinky", jumped into the fray and helped me repel my attackers. Pinky was huge! Pinky and I were a "Mutt and Jeff" combination, to say the least, because he towered over me, standing 6'4", and weighing 250 pounds. Pinky was at the top of the heap in the sophomore class, and he too had gone through, and was still going through, the same moronic process I found myself.

44

Three teachers witnessed both of these after school events. In spite of being jumped by three guys one day, and four guys the next, I was suspended three days for fighting! My reputation was now firmly established. I was labeled a trouble maker, and the reports sent to my parents repeatedly stated this fact.

[It would be terribly dishonest to say I do not still harbor some ill-will toward the teachers who turned their backs on my plight. I harbor that same ill-will today too, whenever I contact school board administrators, principals, vice-principals, or teachers, after hearing they are ignoring the plight of a kid being bullied or mistreated. Truly, my contempt and outrage over their lack of concern or action is palpable.]

Pinky and I were kindred spirits in many ways. Although he was not a scholastic giant, Pinky was not a mindless person either. Mostly, we were similar, because no matter the circumstance, Pinky was a fair kid, who simply did not like the fact that four thugs tried to do what neither of them could do alone. From that point on, Pinky and I were inseparable.

The sad thing about our relationship, however, was even though Pinky clearly sat atop the sophomore class, and I had clearly worked my way to the top of the freshman class, whether I wanted to be there or not, challenges never stopped. When a single challenger approached one of us, which was a daily event, one would step aside, and allow the other to defend himself. If more than one challenger came along though, we would stand side-by-side, or back-to-back, and defended ourselves. There simply was no other way to exist.

[Again, I am going to state, this sort of behavior/reaction is still going on in schools today: The teachers and administrators KNEW what was taking place, and they did nothing! If punishments were meted-out, the defenders were punished along with the instigators. This was, and remains, shameful.]

During the seventh week of school, Pinky and I walked out of the school, and eight relentless losers jumped us. Much to our surprise, another sophomore, who had lost fights against Pinky any number of times, jumped into the fight – on our side – and the three of us walked away from eight bodies lying on the grounds surrounding West Tech's South doorway. Ron had now joined our team, and we three, through no choice of our own, were now considered a gang! (That word, gang, was not used the same as it is today. We were just three people defending each other).

While all of this was going on at school, things at home were miserable. Because of the trouble at school, and the lack of support from witnessing teachers, the news my parents heard was bleak. They reacted accordingly. Sadly, while I just wanted to be left alone, the reality to it all was that leaving things alone was not in my mother's bag of tricks.

Mom knew something was wrong with her "baby", but she could not identify what it was (**nor did she ask**). She automatically assumed a great many things, however, believing the mostly false reports from school.

Because of her assumptions, she nagged and lectured endlessly about things so irrelevant I could not stand being around her. She never asked ME what was happening at school. Never! She never asked what was troubling me, either. Although I tried to explain what was happening, my accounting differed tremendously from what she read in the reports from school. She assumed that I must be doing something wrong, because I was "always in trouble", and in her assumptions, she lectured, and I tuned her out!

In hindsight, the saddest thing was the fact that (until my first day of high school) I had never been in any trouble whatsoever. Oh, I misbehaved on occasion, but trouble – real trouble? Never! I was a good kid. I loved playing sports and being with my friends. I was in two actual fights before going into high school. One fight was in the eighth grade with a friend named Bill, and to this day, I don't know what Bill was mad about.

Because there was no haven at home though, I started hanging out as far from there as I could. Pinky and Ron both had fake ID's, so together we three began frequenting a place called, "The Corner Bar". I was fourteen when I first walked into The Corner Bar and started drinking 3.2% beer. I was a frequent patron of the bar too, so by the time I was seventeen, I was served my drink of choice: Bourbon straight, with a beer chaser. I escaped as best I could.

During my freshman year, the basketball coach from my old grade school quit, and the school needed someone to coach the team. At 4'10" tall, aside from being suspended from all athletic endeavors, I was too short to play basketball in high school. This, however, was an opportunity to get away from home in the evenings (for practices) and on Saturday's (when the games were played). With my dad's support, I volunteered to coach the basketball team at St. Boniface, and the school officials allowed it! We won a lot of games that year, even making it to the city championship series. In that sole endeavor, I found tremendous joy, and a safe haven. I relished in the success of "my team". Unfortunately, the school found an adult to coach the team in 1964, and I was once again left to my own devices. How I loved coaching!

At any rate, as if fighting with students and gangs within the school wasn't enough, one of my teachers called me a, "Stupid Son-of-a-bitch", because I could not comprehend his instructions, and asked for help. I would not abide by that slur, and I demanded an apology. When no apology was forthcoming, and the insult was actually repeated, the teacher and I had a physical encounter. Immediately following our altercation, I walked to the Vice-Principal's office, where I was already very well known.

As you might imagine, I had already grown very bitter by this point in time, and my actions were now reflecting that bitterness. According to my report card, I missed 46 complete days of classes during the first half of the 9th grade. Admittedly, I had also grown weary of the daily battles, so I did cut classes on occasion. 38 of those missed days, however, were because I was suspended for defending myself. I knew the Assistant Vice-Principal of the 9th grade very well.

Normally, a teacher would phone the office as a student went to see the VP. In some cases, the teacher would escort the student to the office, in order to report an offense. In this case, I walked into the Vice-Principal's outer office, sat across from his secretary, and waited for my knocked-out teacher to wake up and report the incident. In spite of his actions, the teacher was never reprimanded. I was suspended for three weeks. There was talk of my being expelled, but when student witnesses came forward and testified about the events, expulsion was shelved. I was still suspended from all classes for fifteen days though, and I was permanently removed from this particular class for the rest of the year.

Because of missed time, I failed most of my freshman classes. The second half was a repeat of the first, and I attended summer school, day and night, to make-up most of the missed second half. I think the accelerated pace of those alternative courses challenged me, and since none of my antagonists were present, I passed all of my classes and almost fully rejoined my peers our sophomore year.

During the summer, as I attended those classes, I determined I was not going to allow my sophomore year to be a repeat of my freshman debacle. I was trying to straighten matters out at home too, with mild successes here and there. Mom's lecturing was incessant though, and I truly did detest hearing the same things over and over, especially when she did not believe what was happening. I avoided her at all cost. I still detest assumptions, and I remain more than willing to engage anyone falsely accusing another of misconduct without facts!

In the summer between the first and second year of high school, something very odd took place at home. I wondered about this event for decades:

One day, I received a phone call from my cousin Jerry. Jerry was ten years older than me. Although we did things together as a family, I had never really gone anywhere or done anything one-on-one with my cousin. During this phone call, however, Jerry asked if I'd like to "hang" with him on the following Saturday, and I consented, wondering what he had in mind.

The following Saturday, Jerry picked me up, and for the next number of hours, he took me to some of the most disgusting places I had ever been. We visited some of his "friends", and what I saw were apartments without furniture; with beds thrown on the floor, along with filthy clothing, garbage, urine and feces. These places were repulsive, and although Jerry was a rogue, I would never have imagined these people were really close associates. I knew I was way out of my element, and I wanted to go home. Finally, after visiting five different apartments, each worse than the previous, Jerry dropped me off at home, and left without saying a word.

For years I wondered, "What the hell was that about?"

About two years before she died, I was home visiting my Aunt Lou (Cleveland will always be home), and I asked her about that day. I asked if she remembered the situation, and her response was immediate, and affirmative! She remembered it vividly.

"OK, then, would you please tell me what that was all about?" I asked.

My Aunt's reply floored me. She said, "We wanted you to stop taking drugs, so we had Jerry take you to visit the heroin and cocaine addicts he knew. We wanted to show where your actions were taking you!" I was stunned!

I had never touched drugs of any sort in my life (other than cigarettes – and by then, alcohol). For them to assume I was involved with drugs totally horrified me. When I explained the reality of my situation, Aunt Lou stared at me for a long moment, and then we laughed. When the fullness of it all set in though, we cried. I was going through puberty, and I was becoming sexually active. That is where my "interest" was. Sex – Yes! Drugs – Absolutely NOT!

My family had made some terrible assumptions, but instead of asking me, or having an older cousin ask; we all paid a terrible price.

49

Pinky, Ron and I saw each other occasionally at The Corner Bar that summer, but each of us was trying to enjoy our time away from school. Aside from attending summer school, I had two part-time jobs, making casual visiting very unpractical.

By the first day of my sophomore year, I had grown a full twelve inches. At 5'10", weighing about 180 pounds, I was considerably larger than the first day of my freshman year. I no longer looked like a freak, but having already acquired my reputation, there was no turning back. Pinky was still massive, and Ron had grown to 6'1". He weighed 175 pounds. We had changed. We had aged a bit. And we had renewed hope that things would be better this year.

To our dismay, the battles began again as we left school the first day! Although the fights of that year were not as frequent, they came frequently enough to mess with my plans – and my grades. Weekly battles, and one or two day suspensions, were commonplace... Although I maintained the course, I again attended summer school day and night in the summer of 1965. Football was entirely lost to me by this time though, and I hated everything and nearly everyone!

The fall of 1965 was no different. Day one, we were jumped by another group. We were surprised though, when the new senior class, of which Pinky was no longer a member, approached us, making it clear they were not about to allow the three of us to rule their turf. Rule turf? Hell, all we wanted was to be left alone. "Oh, please, just go away!"

Fred and many of his classmates whom I had known for years, had graduated in 1965, so this older group was untethered by any loyalties to that older class.

Confronting us at that moment though, was a very interesting situation. While we were not about to be bullied by anyone without a fight, we were vastly outnumbered, and for the first time I had serious doubts about our well-being. What took place over the next fifteen minutes, however, is one of the funniest memories I have from High School. (Sadly, there weren't many funny memories from that period!)

As it turned out, a senior, also named Ron, and a junior girl, named Connie, came to our aid. The five of us, although ultimately battered, stood our ground and fended off this assault. Ron II was almost as big as Pinky. Perhaps 6'3" and weighing about 220 pounds, this kid could handle himself!

Connie, however, could not have been taller than 4'2", and if she weighed more than ninety pounds, I would have been surprised. Weight and height aside though, Connie kicked some serious butt. She was fearless! I had never met a girl like her before, or since. Single-handedly, or actually, with one foot, Connie eliminated three guys from the fight, catching them by surprise from the rear! Once the remaining seniors realized what was happening, one of them hit her very hard, knocking her out. He immediately received my full attention. While I was occupied with this one kid, Pinky and the Ron's took care of the other four seniors still standing.

Later that afternoon, as Connie and I sat together talking about the day, (icing her left jaw), she confided that she had wanted to talk with me throughout the previous two years, but she was too shy. She also told me she had wanted to help during that first year, especially when I was outnumbered, but she was too afraid. She had decided over the summer though, that if it happened again, and she saw me in trouble, she would help, "No matter what!"

Connie proved she was more than capable on that first day. Not surprisingly, this very cute young lady became my girlfriend, and we dated for the remainder of my time at West Tech.

And so it was. And so it continued for a number of months. Because of the fights, defending ourselves, as witnessed by MANY teachers and administrators, we were all suspended regularly. Sadly, because of the suspensions, my mother had another brilliant idea on how she was going to "straighten-out" her troubled son.

That statement alone should tip you off to the fact that things on the home front were worse than ever. My relationship with my mother was in total disarray. At that point in my life, "I absolutely hated her guts". This might sound harsh and extreme, but in truth, I am pulling my punch, and I am holding back. I loathed her! And, I wanted absolutely nothing to do with her, her nagging, or her lectures.

And kids today don't think we understand, while in truth, many of us do!

The saddest thing to me was that my relationship with my dad was not great either. The man, whom I adored and longed to spend all of my time with, did not know how to reach out to me, and I could not connect with him either. No matter how hard we tried, the strain of my relationship with mom pressed in on us, and we grew apart.

We had a caricature of my dad, which portrayed him as a very large bear with a rose in its mouth. And in truth, that was my dad. Discipline, therefore, was not his forte'. While dad would sit and try to talk through something, it was my mother who was the disciplinarian, and at times, in that vein, she was imaginative!.

Talking about my dad with my cousin Denise recently, she used a word to describe my father that I had never considered before. Her assessment of him was amazingly astute though. She called him a person who enjoyed extreme "Carefreeness". She could not have been more correct. Denise, by the way, is an individual who enjoys an extreme case of "carefreeness" today, and because she reminds me so much of my dad, my time with her, these days, is always outstanding!

Contributing further to the strain at home, however, was that my relationship with my brother had deteriorated too. Before delving into a conversation about Fred though, I will tell you about the second of my two elementary school fights, because this will explain exactly what I mean by being willing to engage: During the summer of 1962, between the 7th and 8th grades, I learned a valuable lesson with regard to defending oneself. I have since entitled that lesson, "Willingness". In a nutshell, we are either willing to fight for what we believe, or we are not. We are either willing to defend ourselves, or we are not. Size is almost irrelevant in many fights, as Connie proved repeatedly, (and as a very vocal minority in our country is repeatedly proving today), because willingness, more often than not, rules.

Willingness rules!

I never knew how to back down. BUT, that does not mean I was never afraid. Fear and backing down is not the same thing. We must learn the truth of that fact right now, because being willing to engage simply means we manage our fear, and press on in spite of that fear!

The lesson I learned that summer, was unless I was willing to have the money in my pocket stolen, I had to be willing to stand up against a bully. I had to be willing to engage, even if that meant getting my butt kicked. I was working part-time at two delicatessens in the evenings and weekends, cleaning and restocking shelves and such; things I had done at the F&L Delicatessen since I was four. During that summer, a high school kid, considerably older and much larger than me, decided he was going to steal whatever money was in my possession.

Frankly, I was not willing to surrender my hard earned cash to this bully. I was, however, willing to try and stop him from stealing what was mine. About two hours after our altercation, this young man was dragged to our house by his mother, who demanded reimbursement for her medical expenses from my mom. He required stitches, because I beat the crap out of her kid.

When mom called me to the door and asked for an explanation, the lady looked at my four foot nothing self, and asked her nearly six foot tall son if I was in fact the kid who beat him up. His reply was, "Yes!" I asked if she knew why we fought, and she said, "No!" I threatened her son, "Tell your mother what happened!" Upon hearing the truth, she merely looked at my mom and me, grabbed her kid by the arm, and never darkened our doorstep again.

Through nearly three years of fighting at school, I was "willing" to defend myself, and to that end, I was willing to inflict as much damage as necessary, to insure that my friends and I remained safe. I was not a dirty fighter though! I never hit or kicked anyone who was down on the ground. To quote John Wayne, "A man has to have a code", and I had a code. As long as a person stood fighting against me, I fought back. Once they were down, the matter was settled. Period!

When it came to fighting with my brother, however, I was not "willing"! No matter how angry we had become with each other, I always pulled my punches and opted to half wrestle instead, in the hope that dad, or some other family member, would simply pull us apart and make us go our separate ways.

In spite of my best efforts to change my situation, things simply grew worse daily, and it was in this atmosphere that I clandestinely began meeting with the Army Recruiter in early November of 1965. I was sixteen years old!

Chapter 6 – My Tumultuous Years, Part III

O n the home front, the ultimate insult, or slap in the face, came when my mother, in an act of desperation or vindictiveness (I was never quite certain which), "invited" her brother, my Uncle Ray, to discipline me, to "straighten-him-out".

It was not unusual for Uncle Ray to stop by the house, especially when he was working on the Westside. So, I didn't think anything about seeing his welding truck parked out front when I came home from hanging out with Connie early one afternoon. (We were suspended again). The instant I walked through the door though, he made his intentions known.

My uncle was a big man. At 6'4", and well over 260 pounds, the man had a distinct physical advantage over me, and the 'surprise' of his assault caught me off-guard. We were in our home, after all, and I really did not think he had come to, "kick your ass", as he blurted during his charge.

Thankfully, I was able to push away his initial assault, and for a moment I looked at my mother, and all I saw in her eyes was anger, contempt, frustration, and worst of all, a great deal of fear. The fact that my own mother now feared me truly stunned me.

In hindsight, I realize how severely the impact of this event wounded my heart. I was mortified. I had never harmed a member of my family, and would have fought anyone attempting to harm any one of them. This action, however, contradicted everything we had been told during our elementary school years, because there was no dignity in this. There was no integrity or justice in this. I was being assaulted by a member of my family, and it took years of exchanging letters with mom for most of the wounds of this event to heal.

Nevertheless, I had this raging maniac threatening me, and I was not about to submit to this bully. So, I did what any other "willing" individual would do. I retaliated. I had to think fast though, because at that particular moment, I was at a terrible disadvantage.

Being in the house would have allowed him to corner me too easily, and I was not about to be trapped by this behemoth in close quarters. If you knew my Uncle Ray at that time, you would have known that the man had a jaw of stone, and I was not going to repel his attack in a boxing match. Besides, I did not want to get that close to him. He was taller, he outweighed me, he had a longer reach, and all I had on my side was speed, agility, and that "willingness to engage". I needed to change the setting so things were on a more level playing field.

Knowing my uncle as I did, (having seen him in a state of rage frequently throughout the years), I knew that anger was ruling his actions, and he was not thinking rationally. So, I "called the old man out". Moving toward the front door, I said something about not entirely destroying his sister's house, and, "Did he really want to do this where she might be hurt as well?" I taunted him too, knowing that in his state of mind he would not resist an opportunity to, "Really do this thing he had in mind without restraint". Thankfully he obliged.

After nearly three years of constant battling, I had learned a great deal about defending myself. Being outside was to my advantage. As difficult as this is to write, because of the circumstances, at that particular moment, I too was filled with rage, and I was more than willing to engage. I just needed room to do so.

Once outside, I was able to move, and as he charged toward me, I was able to land the first blow, hitting my uncle as hard as I could in his lower stomach! It was not a cheap shot either! Although he may have been willing, he was getting up there in years, and he had developed quite a gut. I took advantage of his being out of shape. Naturally, being hit as hard as he was, in such a tender spot, he doubled over and fell to the ground.

As soon as he hit the ground, I grabbed a Pepsi bottle that I had set on the porch before entering the house. I was planning on getting my deposit back when I bought a replacement "pop". This bottle, however, was not being returned anywhere, because I broke the bottom off the bottle, on the steps leading to the house. Holding the neck of the now broken bottle in my left hand, I simply told my uncle that unless he was willing to visit the hospital emergency room; his attempt to "kick my ass" was over.

Mom, to say the least, was horrified. Standing on the porch, she screamed at me to not do any more. With tears streaming down my face, I looked at my frightened mother and told her, "I never wanted this!" "I never asked for this!" "I never did anything to deserve this!"

I also told her how much I detested the fact she would ever consider asking this man to 'discipline me'. I had a real man for a father, and this fool was not equal to the task! And, as I walked away, not turning my back to my uncle for an instant, I told her to call off her dog, and to never do anything like that to me again. "Next time, I won't stop!"

At this time I also told my mother I would be moving out as soon as I could make arrangements. I think my statement about moving actually surprised her, but I could not 'read' her reaction at all. Too much had happened too quickly, and the only thing I saw in her face was fear.

I spent the remainder of that day with the Army Recruiter, and Connie, returning home only after I knew dad would be home from work.

My father did not know about the incident earlier in the day, and I did not tell him. I never told him. And, I do not know if my mother ever told him either. Even after mom died, I never mentioned the subject to dad, because it served no purpose whatsoever, and he never mentioned it to me.

Nonetheless, dad and I discussed a number of things that evening, and in the course of our conversation I outlined my plan. I explained that although I was only sixteen, I had signed a Letter of Intent to enlist in the Army that afternoon, but that I needed his support to actually accomplish what else needed to be done. My mother remained in her bedroom while dad and I talked, and in reality, she and I did not see each other, or talk with each other, for more than a few days.

At any rate, within days of signing my Letter of Intent, the Army Recruiter had me included in an already scheduled two-day series of tests, taking place in early December, 1965. Upon passing those tests, I would earn my GED High School Equivalency Diploma. Passing those tests was vital to my enlistment, so failure, under the circumstances, was not an option. Failure would disqualify me from entering the military. The pressure was on – and I knew it.

About two weeks after the exams were taken; the recruiter received a preliminary report from the State of Ohio, informing us that I had passed every test. With that hurdle out of the way, I was eligible to fully enlist in the Army. There was one more hurdle in my path, to be leapt: With a copy of the preliminary results of the GED tests in hand, I sat across the dining room table from my parents, and explained that according to the State of Ohio, I had officially graduated from high school. "My days at West Tech are over," and, "I have other documents for you to sign."

In what was perhaps the first unemotional conversation we had held in nearly three years, I detailed my plan to my parents, (repeating it all for dad). I explained that they either sign the forms I was passing to them, or I was walking out the door "then and now", and "perhaps never returning". "At least this way", I said, "you will know where I am."

My mother contested for only a moment, but then my dad, saying only four words, firmly insisted, "Sign the forms, Laurice!", and with that said, my mother and father signed every document needed, not only for my entry into the Army, but basically for my emancipation as well.

In Chapter Nine of "A Diamond on The Wall", after a series of emotional events, I said, "I recalled years past and times lost," and it was the three years outlined in these chapters that I was referencing. At the same time, I also realized that although I had choices at each step along the way, <u>I was responsible for the choices I made</u>, and in all of these matters, I was neither invincible, nor infallible.

I could easily have remained on the floor that first day of high school, and not struck back. I chose instead to engage and defend. Perhaps through being docile I could have saved myself a tremendous amount of grief, aggravation, pain and suffering, and possibly even saved my family from these as well. ***But, in remaining docile, how susceptible might I have been to other forms of bullying and verbal abuse, because I was deemed a milquetoast or sissy?***

My focus today, however, is with those, who like me, are now – or still – willing to engage, because something is not right, or those who want to learn how to engage in order to protect others now being persecuted. **<u>My focus today is to fortify anyone willing to use the coin in their pocket.</u>** Using our coins, and being who we are meant to be, is what this book is all about.

I cannot alter one instant of my life, and even if I could, I do not believe I would. I had to be true to who and what I was meant to be. I am the person I am today, because of the events and experiences of my life, and although I am not perfect, I am at peace with myself and my Creator. I only hope more people learn to feel and say the same.

Because of the events of my life, and through my studies of Scripture, and my faith, I readily see the decay occurring within our families, and recognize the impact of that decay. I see the continuing, ongoing push of the bullies, and know that we must engage on behalf of their victims, and shut them down. I am observing the unending march of those who wish to destroy our nation as well, and am compelled to make a stand against the idiocy within our government. I am witnessing the onslaught of any number of heinous and hurtful things that people do daily, and I am enraged that a silent majority is permitting those offenses.

I am praying that by exposing the futility of my tumultuous years, I might touch the heart of someone contemplating suicide, and help them know that their lives have purpose, meaning and value.

As a society, we must become willing to engage on every level in order to preserve the value and self-worth of every person. That engagement includes the preservation of our own lives as well. Nothing is free, but then too, nothing else really matters. If we are untrue to ourselves, our lives are a lie, and there is no salvation whatsoever in a false faith or false "religion". That is how base my original philosophy truly is. I hope you might now understand why it has taken so long for me to learn how to fully express and explain it all.

At sixteen I knew I needed to be true to who I was. At sixty-three, I can now boldly say, "We all need to be true to who we really are!"

The unanswered question, however, is, "Are you willing to engage in whatever battle you personally believe needs fighting, in order to realize your full worth?" "Are you willing to take your coin out of your pocket and use it?"

Life is short, and given the chance, most people would treasure the simple opportunity to love and be loved. Unfortunately, we are not being allowed that simple opportunity. Life requires our involvement, and issues of the utmost significance and importance demand our participation.

In truth, we do not need gangs, but gangs exist for three primary reasons: First, someone, somewhere, wants to harm someone else, which forces people to join together for protection. Second, some people simply want to dominate and oppress other people. And third, people need a "family" who will uphold them and give them worth; whether that worth has integrity or dignity, however, is another issue altogether. Gangs exist today, because these very basic elements are now missing in the lives of many, many, people!

These matters require our involvement, and demand our participation.

My "gang" and I simply wanted to be left alone. Instead, we were forced to defend ourselves on a daily basis, and in that defense, we were labeled as incorrigible, truant, trouble-makers and every other slanderous label that folks wanted to place on us.

When the elders of my family turned against me, Pinky, Ron I, Ron II and Connie became my family. When my relatives attacked, instead of protecting, and when authorities refused to tell the truth and stand up against the bullies, I turned to other sources for protection.

We must learn to implement logical, common sense solutions to the issues of our day, but the only way common sense is ever going to return to our society, is IF the silent majority of civil, honest, sincere citizens, worldwide, become "Willing To Engage". The very vocal minority will hate every logical, common sense solution offered, but the time has come for the silent majority to reclaim ownership of this nation. To that end the following chapters are dedicated.

The only difference between me and many kids today, is the fact that Divine intervention is a reality, and it was "meant to be" that through my experiences, my Father in Heaven might allow me to reach out and help at least one kid or parent who is troubled today.

Sadly, when I obtained my GED and technically finished high school, my "gang" abandoned me and wanted nothing further to do with me. I never heard from or saw any of them again. On the flip-side though, entering the Army and growing in a very disciplined and structured atmosphere, helped me regain the real family I had somehow lost.

And, it would be unfair of me not to add that through our very frequent exchange of letters, my mom and I were able to openly and freely talk about my high school years, and the events that took place. Without the stress and contradicting information, she finally listened and believed what I had been trying to tell her. With this understanding in mind, my mom, Uncle Ray and I sat together and talked for some time while I was on leave, on my way to Vietnam from Germany. During that conversation they both apologized for the events of November, 1965, while I apologized for the disrespect and contempt that was in my heart. I left for Vietnam with my family intact.

As a whole, therefore, I fervently believe we need to rethink our approach toward bullies and those who taunt others. We have to change how we deal with them.

We need to rethink our approach toward discipline in general as well.

We need to rethink our involvement (or lack thereof) in daily life, because left unchanged, our path is bleak.

The nature and description of "bullying" varies a great deal within our minds and hearts, and the impact of being bullied is as diverse. In some ways, bullying can be subliminal, thereby making us unaware that we are even being bullied. Consider the evening news: Upon hearing something often enough, we either believe the totality of what we are being told, or we tune out the drone of the topic. And, whether you believe it or not, that type of assault on our senses is a kind of bullying; it is a kind of conditioning.

In my first, "Inspirational Reflections – Food for Thought", which follows this chapter; I discuss conditioning in a way you may never have heard. I hope you enjoy the analogy. Please keep this subliminal conditioning issue in mind though, as you read that story, because it applies to our lives today in many ways.

Upon hearing a message delivered from different sources, in many different ways, we either accept that message completely, or we tune out the drone of it all and withdraw. Withdrawal, in case you did not know, is common to most people who have been bullied.

Also common to the victims of bullying is their struggle to maintain their personal value and self-worth. Believe it or not, the silent majority is as they are, because they (WE) have been bullied into subjection and silence.

That said; the remainder of this book is dedicated to two things: First, I am hoping to reestablish the fullness of value and self-worth within the hearts, minds and souls of every person I possibly can. Second, I am hoping to sound a "Call-To-Arms" to the silent majority, from an unknown source (me). I am hoping to act as an encourager to each person, that we would become "Willing To Engage" and be "Silent No More!" We must find the strength and courage to unite against the bullies in defense of, and on behalf of, ourselves, our families, our nation, and our world.

We cannot afford to remain silent anymore in regard to matters that will negatively and significantly impact us in the very near future.

I was willing to make radical changes in my life in defense of my very self, because I knew I could do better. I knew I could be better. I knew I had self-worth and value, and in this writing I am hoping to convey those same truths to you. The lessons I learned are offered here for you. I pray that you find it all worthy of your time.

You, most certainly, are worthy of mine!

(Thomas Jefferson)

"What country can preserve its liberties if its rulers are not warned from time to time that their people preserve the spirit of resistance?"

MY THOUGHTS IN PASSING:

Perhaps this brief summary will assist any who might be confused by the primary differences between the liberal left and the conservative right, as they exist today!

Succinctly put, every big-government, entitlement oriented, uncontrolled spending, and narcissistic self-gratifying individual, who is looking for a hand-out from that big government, comprise what is known as the liberal left. Conservative thought, stands in complete opposition to these positions.

As a conservative, for instance, I am as concerned about the environment as any liberal — perhaps even more so! Examples: I will not hug a tree, but I am all for proper forestry management, which insures millions of healthy trees. I will not lay down my life to "save a whale", but I will use my voice in defense of the whales, while giving my life to "Save an Unborn Human Baby".

Conservative thought, in my eyes, conserves. Liberal thought, however, grants with liberality, while presenting a false-face of conservancy, as they pursue their own personal gain and self-serving interests... The differences are huge, and it's time America wakes up!

INSPIRATIONAL REFLECTIONS – FOOD FOR THOUGHT #1:

HOW HAVE YOU BEEN CONDITIONED?

Have you ever heard how they train elephants to remain tethered to a small stake pounded into the ground, thereby stopping them from merely walking away? Considering the size and strength of an elephant, haven't you ever wondered why they don't just pull out the stake and go wherever they want?

When an elephant is young, the trainers clamp a large steel bracelet around one of its hind legs and, connected by a very large steel chain, they secure the baby elephant to a steel stake driven deeply into the ground. Try as it might, the baby elephant cannot break loose from this bondage. For days it will pull and pull, but with decreasing frequency. Eventually, the baby elephant will surrender in defeat. The baby elephant **KNOWS** it cannot break free, so it stops trying.

From that point onward, a simple leather strap replaces the steel bracelet, and whenever the elephants are to be tethered, the leather strap, connected by a small rope, is secured to a wooden peg driven a couple of feet into the ground. The elephant will not pull the peg out though, because as soon as it feels the slightest tug on its leg, it surrenders. Although it is capable of pulling down the circus tent, it will not pull a puny wooden peg out of the ground. It has been conditioned!

So, the question for each of us is: "How have I been conditioned?"

In what way, or in what area of your life, have you been conditioned to believe that you cannot accomplish something that you are, or were, actually meant to do, or that you truly desire to accomplish?

Or, what is it that brings joy to your life, that you do not do anymore, or have never done, because you have been told, "You are not good enough," "You are not trained enough," or, "You are unqualified to accomplish the task"?

Or, how many opportunities have been presented to you, or offered, and not taken, because of fear, or because you thought you were undeserving, or because you were conditioned to believe that you were incapable, or that it was too good to be true?

Have you buried your coin, or are you using it?

Conditioning is so very subtle and insidious that you may not even recognize that you have in fact been conditioned to view things, or to react to things, differently than what might be your natural bent or inclination.

Whatever it might be, when was the last time you did that thing which naturally brings joy to your heart? If there has been a lapse in time, when was the last time you asked yourself, "Why?"

Or, have you never known what it is that truly brings happiness or joy to your life? How very sad!

Perhaps my greatest single strength – or – perhaps my greatest single weakness is that, "I never knew how to back down, so I plowed through!" Somewhere along the path of my life I became conditioned to not give up. I do not know how to quit. I do not know how to surrender.

And I must confess that my inability to surrender has caused tremendous personal grief and pain at times, because I have made myself endure horrible situations much longer than necessary. I know that in each instance, some other person, or some group of people, were impacted positively, because I "stuck-it-out". But in those instances I knew exactly why I could not quit. As painful as it might have been for me and my family personally, my "tenacity" has, in many instances, brought relief to others, and that relief has somehow made it all worthwhile. That is how I am built. That is how I am conditioned.

Perhaps somewhere along the path of your life, you were conditioned to give up and surrender when things got difficult.

Personally, I do not view that type of conditioning as positive. That is why I believe the story I am telling, and the motivation I am offering, is so important. Unless we become willing to engage in our lives, and remain silent no more, I think we will find too many coins buried or hidden, and too many lives lived without joy, happiness, or completeness.

And that would be a horrible waste. Don't you think?

(Thomas Jefferson)

"Timid men prefer the calm of despotism to the tempestuous sea of liberty."

(Abraham Lincoln)

"America will never be destroyed from the outside. If we falter and lose our freedoms, it will be because we destroyed ourselves."

(Abraham Lincoln)

"Any people anywhere, being inclined and having the power, have the right to rise up, and shake off the existing government, and form a new one that suits them better. This is a most valuable – a most sacred right – a right, which we hope and believe, is to liberate the world."

(Abraham Lincoln)

"We the people are the rightful masters of both Congress and the courts, not to overthrow the Constitution but to overthrow the men who pervert the Constitution."

(Abraham Lincoln)

"This country, with its institutions, belongs to the people who inhabit it. Whenever they shall grow weary of the existing government, they can exercise their constitutional right of amending it, or exercise their revolutionary right to overthrow it."

INSPIRATIONAL REFLECTIONS – FOOD FOR THOUGHT #2:

THE SEVEN COW WOMAN!

T here is an old story told, which I try to pass along, to women especially, when I learn that a young girl, a young woman or a grown woman has been psychologically, physically and/or emotionally beaten down throughout their life - - - And I want to offer that old story here for you:

Back in the late 1800's there was a very wealthy Polynesian king who had one son. Being the son of the King, this young man could have chosen for his bride, any one of the young ladies within his father's kingdom. And there were many very beautiful young ladies within his father's kingdom.

The son, however, was in love with a very plain, ordinary and even, in many eyes, a downright homely appearing girl. No matter how hard the king pressed his son to choose another young girl though, the son would not budge in his choice.

It was customary in those days for the father of the groom to negotiate the value of the young lady with her father, and pay a dowry for the right of his son to wed the daughter. And, as was customary, the king visited the father of the chosen maiden to negotiate the dowry.

As the two men sat together, with the son sitting behind his father the king, the negotiations began, and the maiden's father, knowing the plainness and ordinariness of his daughter, asked for one chicken in exchange for the girl. Before the king could respond, however, the son whispered into his father's ear the price they must pay for the maiden, and honoring his sons wishes, the king responded, "No, we will pay a dowry of seven cows for your daughter".

Now it must be understood that payment of one or even two cows for a maiden was considered exceptionally high. Although pleased by such an offer, the father of the maiden questioned the offered value, wondering if the value being set was too high. Nonetheless, the king's son whispered again into his father's ear, insisting that nothing less than seven cows be paid for the young girl.

The father of the young girl had no choice but to accept the price offered. After all, he was dealing with the king. Completing negotiations, a contract was written and sealed, and a wedding date was set. At the appointed time, the entire kingdom waited anxiously to see whether the king's son would actually pay seven cows for the girl, or if the entire matter was merely a cruel hoax.

But, true to his word, the king's son arrived at the maidens village with seven robust and gorgeous cows, all adorned with beautiful harnesses, and wearing the most harmonious bells, which chimed their arrival at the maiden's humble cottage. Upon delivering the seven cows to the father, the king's son and his betrothed were wed, and immediately set off for a year-long honeymoon, traveling aboard a sailing ship awaiting their departure in the harbor.

At the end of a year of traveling and visiting many countries, the vessel arrived in the harbor of the king's islands. With great fanfare every person in the kingdom looked for the groom and his bride. Seeing the groom, they all wondered where the bride was.

As the king's son disembarked, he was accompanied by the most gorgeous woman anyone on the islands had ever seen. There was a great commotion amongst the people, especially between the king and the maiden's father, because his plain, ordinary, and even homely looking daughter could not be seen anywhere.

Outraged, the maiden's father approached the king, insisting an explanation. At the same time the protests were happening, the son and the beautiful woman he was escorting, approached and bowed to the king. Again, the maiden's father insisted on knowing where his daughter had been taken.

Then, for the first time, much to the surprise of everyone present, the beautiful woman standing beside the king's son began speaking to her father. She identified herself to him, to the king, and to the people of the kingdom.

Astonished, the maiden's father, and the king himself, asked how such a transformation could take place. How could such a plain, ordinary and homely maiden be transformed into such a beautiful woman?

Bowing humbly, the son simply explained that throughout her life everyone, her father included, had treated the girl as if she were a one chicken woman; as if she were in fact plain, ordinary and homely. But he saw the fullness of her beauty, and paid seven cows for what he knew to be her true worth.

Then, over the course of their year-long honeymoon, he proved to her every day, by word and deed, that she was in fact a seven cow woman.

Once she began to believe her husband, she began to act as if she was, in fact, a seven cow woman.

And the fullness of her transformed heart, as a person, was the gorgeous woman standing before the king, her father, and the entire kingdom that day.

Ladies, in case you have never been told – YOU are a seven cow woman!

No matter what has been said to you over the years; no matter what has been done to you over the years; no matter how homely, plain, useless, or valueless you feel, in the eyes of the Son of the King, you are all seven cow women. No one can ever steal the truth or fullness of that value from you!

YOU ARE A SEVEN COW WOMAN.

ALL THAT WE NEED NOW –

IS FOR YOU TO BELIEVE!

(Copyright © 2012 Jimmy Hagewood)
"Knowledge is good, but knowledge properly applied is wisdom. It's good to have the will to try, but we must take action and do. The time to be better is now! Be better by helping others be their best! Do it every day and DO IT BIG!!!"

Photograph Library

Larry - 4, feeding his Squirrel

Larry 9

Fred 10

Fred & Larry – in back row, with cousins
Marc – and *his sister,*
Denise (The Holy Terror of the Vosen Family).

Just look at THAT face, and you will have some idea as to what dealing with *her* was like back then. *She* is 6 years younger than me!

I have stories about *her* alone that would curdle your hair and have you laughing in the aisles. What a brat!

Denise (Ever the brat) – 2011
At an Indian's game in Cleveland
with Larry

Larry, leaning against our Austin Healey A40 Van, and Freddy-boy with his new Schwinn Bike.

I wish we had both – in mint condition today!

Mom, me, Freddy-boy and Dad

Our Mom! – Laurice Vosen

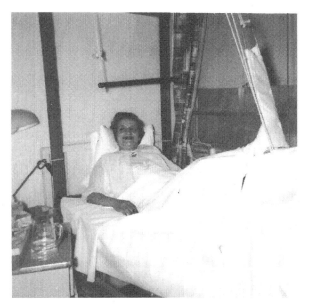

Mom recovering from major surgery
in May of 1952.

I was 3-1/2 when this was taken, and
the window to her left is where she waved
to us from, as we sat in a rowboat

on a small lake off Liberty Boulevard.

Larry - Standing, with
Sister-in-Law, Mona and
Brother, Fred
Summer 2011

Charlie & Larry - 2010

Larry Vosen; Fall 2011

Uncle Ed
Cousin Jerry
Uncle John (Lt. Colonel John Shalala)
Uncle Rusty

And Yes, if you are trying to connect the name, Donna Shalala (From the Clinton Administration) is John Shalala's niece. Donna's dad and my Uncle John were brothers.

Like I said, I come from a very interesting family! Further proof of that is in the next photo…

I simply could not write this book without telling you about Fifi, a very special character in our family...

I only wish I could show this in color.

As I have said many times, I come from a crazy and hilarious family, and here is the topping of that "fruitcake"... My mom and dad dreamt up this skit as a practical joke very early-on in the 1960's.

My grandfather (Jiddu), whose eyesight was not the greatest, though, fell in love with Fifi, and would always anxiously inquire as to whether Fifi had been invited to a party. Obligingly, Fifi always 'popped-in' for a short visit.

Fifi and Denise (background left) are both staring at Jiddu, who I am told, was reacting very joyously to Fifi's visit.

Fifi, in case you cannot tell, is my dad – in drag!

His dress is a very light purple with four bands of gold frill. His necklace is turquoise, the feather is pink, his wig is white, and completing his outfit was a pair of golden slippers.

Ever the entertainer, Fifi would sing a song or two, in a very sweet falsetto voice, always sitting on Jiddu's lap for a while, tickling him with "her" feather.

And, as you might imagine, we would howl and applaud...

MY THOUGHTS IN PASSING:

"Whatever happened to self-worth? Whatever happened to contributing to the good of society? Whatever happened to simple folks, working hard in order to live good and decent lives, without the government interfering in, or with those lives? Where is the value in what we are doing, or allowing to be done, and what are we teaching the next generations if we allow this pandering to continue?"

"In any conversation about our national debt though, we must also DEMAND that all monies "borrowed" from the Social Security and Medicare Funds, be repaid – with interest. The national debt today, for which we are in fact paying interest, does not include these stolen monies, but we must mandate the correction of the unconscionable theft from our retirement and medical care insurance funds. "We the People" paid for these insurances, but because of horrible mismanagement by an entitlement driven political machine, our systems, and our citizens are now suffering."

INSPIRATIONAL REFLECTIONS – FOOD FOR THOUGHT #3:

OATHS OF SERVICE:

✓ The following is the official Oath of Allegiance that must be taken by all immigrants who wish to become United States Citizens:

"I hereby declare, on oath, that I absolutely and entirely renounce and abjure all allegiance and fidelity to any foreign prince, potentate, state or sovereignty, of whom or which I have heretofore been a subject or citizen; that I will support and defend the Constitution and laws of the United States of America against all enemies, foreign and domestic; that I will bear true faith and allegiance to the same; that I will bear arms on behalf of the United States when required by the law; that I will perform noncombatant service in the armed forces of the United States when required by the law; that I will perform work of national importance under civilian direction when required by the law; and that I take this obligation freely without any mental reservation or purpose of evasion; so help me God."

Note: If a person can provide enough evidence that their religious training and beliefs prevent them from saying certain language within the Oath of Allegiance, provisions are provided – and instructions are given, so that a person does not need to violate their training and beliefs.

✓ Oath of Enlistment into the Armed Forces of the United States:

I, *(NAME)*, do solemnly swear (or affirm) that I will support and defend the Constitution of the United States against all enemies, foreign and domestic; that I will bear true faith and allegiance to the same; and that I will obey the orders of the President of the United States and the orders of the officers appointed over me, according to regulations and the Uniform Code of Military Justice. So help me God.

✓ Oath of Enlistment into the National Guard:

I, *(NAME)*, do solemnly swear (or affirm) that I will support and defend the Constitution of the United States and the State of *(STATE NAME)* against all enemies, foreign and domestic; that I will bear true faith and allegiance to the same; and that I will obey the orders of the President of the United States and the Governor of *(STATE NAME)* and the orders of the officers appointed over me, according to law and regulations. So help me God.

Please note in the reading of these oaths, that there is NO expiration date affixed to them. There is no end to the duration of the oath. I think that is significant, don't you?

✓ Federal Executive and Legislative Branch Oaths:

In the United States, the oath of office for the President is specified in the Constitution (Article II, Section 1):

"I do solemnly swear (or affirm) that I will faithfully execute the Office of President of the United States, and will to the best of my Ability, preserve, protect and defend the Constitution of the United States."

The oath may be sworn or affirmed (in which case it is called an *affirmation* instead of *oath*). Although not present in the text of the Constitution, it is customary for modern presidents to say "So help me God" after the end of the oath. For officers other than the President, the expression "So help me God" is explicitly prescribed, but the Judiciary Act of 1789 also explains when it can be omitted (specifically for oaths taken by court clerks): "Which words, so help me God, shall be omitted in all cases where an affirmation is admitted instead of an oath."

The Constitution (Article VI, clause 3) also specifies:

The Senators and Representatives before mentioned, and the members of the several state legislatures, and all executive and judicial officers, both of the United States and of the several states, shall be bound by oath or affirmation, to support this Constitution; but no religious test shall ever be required as a qualification to any office or public trust under the United States.

At the start of each new U.S. Congress, in January of every odd-numbered year, newly elected or re-elected Members of Congress – the entire House of Representatives and one-third of the Senate – must recite an oath:

"I do solemnly swear (or affirm) that I will support and defend the Constitution of the United States against all enemies, foreign and domestic; that I will bear true faith and allegiance to the same; that I take this obligation freely, without any mental reservation or purpose of evasion; and that I will well and faithfully discharge the duties of the office on which I am about to enter. So help me God."

This oath is also taken by the Vice President, members of the Cabinet, federal judges and all other civil and military officers and federal employees other than the President.

(Thomas Jefferson – *Quoting Cesare Beccaria*)
"Laws that forbid the carrying of arms...disarm only those who are neither inclined nor determined to commit crimes... Such laws make things worse for the assaulted and better for the assailants; they serve rather to encourage than to prevent homicides, for an unarmed man may be attacked with greater confidence than an armed man."

(Thomas Jefferson)
"The beauty of the Second Amendment is that it will not be needed until they try to take it."

(Thomas Jefferson)
"I predict future happiness for Americans if they can prevent the government from wasting the labors of the people under the pretense of taking care of them."

INSPIRATIONAL REFLECTIONS – FOOD FOR THOUGHT #4:

THE BILL OF RIGHTS:

The following text is a transcription of the first ten amendments to the Constitution in their original form. These amendments were ratified on December 15, 1791, and form what is known as the "Bill of Rights."

Amendment I

Congress shall make no law respecting an establishment of religion, or prohibiting the free exercise thereof; or abridging the freedom of speech, or of the press; or the right of the people peaceably to assemble, and to petition the Government for a redress of grievances.

Amendment II

A well regulated Militia, being necessary to the security of a free State, the right of the people to keep and bear Arms, shall not be infringed.

Amendment III

No Soldier shall, in time of peace be quartered in any house, without the consent of the Owner, nor in time of war, but in a manner to be prescribed by law.

Amendment IV

The right of the people to be secure in their persons, houses, papers, and effects, against unreasonable searches and seizures, shall not be violated, and no Warrants shall issue, but upon probable cause, supported by Oath or affirmation, and particularly describing the place to be searched, and the persons or things to be seized.

Amendment V

No person shall be held to answer for a capital, or otherwise infamous crime, unless on a presentment or indictment of a Grand Jury, except in cases arising in the land or naval forces, or in the Militia, when in actual service in time of War or public danger; nor shall any person be subject for the same offence to be twice put in jeopardy of life or limb; nor shall be compelled in any criminal case to be a witness against himself, nor be deprived of life, liberty, or property, without due process of law; nor shall private property be taken for public use, without just compensation.

Amendment VI

In all criminal prosecutions, the accused shall enjoy the right to a speedy and public trial, by an impartial jury of the State and district wherein the crime shall have been committed, which district shall have been previously ascertained by law, and to be informed of the nature and cause of the accusation; to be confronted with the witnesses against him; to have compulsory process for obtaining witnesses in his favor, and to have the Assistance of Counsel for his defence.

Amendment VII

In Suits at common law, where the value in controversy shall exceed twenty dollars, the right of trial by jury shall be preserved, and no fact tried by a jury, shall be otherwise re-examined in any Court of the United States, than according to the rules of the common law.

Amendment VIII

Excessive bail shall not be required, nor excessive fines imposed, nor cruel and unusual punishments inflicted.

Amendment IX

The enumeration in the Constitution, of certain rights, shall not be construed to deny or disparage others retained by the people.

Amendment X

The powers not delegated to the United States by the Constitution, nor prohibited by it to the States, are reserved to the States respectively, or to the people.

Chapter 7 – Let Us Then Begin

You now know what my tumultuous years were like. You now know why I did, what I did, with regard to leaving home at such an early age and joining the Army. You also now know how I feel about people on a one-by-one basis; that every person has tremendous value and worth, and how I believe that each person deserves to be treated with respect – and even more, with true love.

I am in possession of an essay; a homework assignment actually, written by a young friend of mine, named Bradley. I am offering Bradley's (unedited) essay here for your consideration. I will present my thoughts afterward:

"My Grandpa Larry"

My great friend Larry is like my grandpa because he is one of the older people in my life and has been there for me when I needed help, since I was 7 years old. Both of my biological grandpas have already passed away and he really filled a hole. One of the reasons that I like Larry a lot is that he wrote a book of his memoirs of being a Green Beret in Vietnam during the war. I learned many things from his stories.

I said before that Larry had written a book; it is called *A Diamond on The Wall*. While he was writing the book, I read through the chapters to help find any errors, add more imagery, or just make it understandable to someone else who doesn't know him. He was only eighteen and a half when his boots touched the dirt of that foreign country of Vietnam during 1967 – 1968. He was barely 17 years old when he had enlisted, (with his parents' signatures) and entered the Army. After boot camp, he spent time in Germany before being sent to South Vietnam. It's a great book and I highly recommend it. I have learned many things about life and camaraderie from his stories.

Some of the things that he has taught me I think every man should act like and go by. He has taught me to hold doors open for people, don't talk down to or about others, and simply respect everyone as if they are your brothers or sisters. Sometimes it can be really hard because there are the few that just have no respect for me or my family and friends. I try really hard to ignore them, which is what I've been taught to do if at all possible. Another one of the big things I have learned is to respect women no matter what. Also, to live life to the fullest and keep your glass half full. People need to know they are valuable. I like the old fashioned values of respecting those around you. Everyone is important. It's a John Wayne thing. A man's got to have a creed to live by.

I was really interested in learning about Larry's past as a young man and what he's done and gone through in his life. It meant a lot to me that he asked me to help him with reading and editing it. Since Larry is like my grandpa, it was very important to me that he'd asked for my opinion.

This is a great book for those interested in facts of the Vietnam War, an auto-biography of a young Green Beret or growing up in the 1960's. It has been great getting to know Larry as I grow up. I haven't been able to see him lately, since he's recently moved to Las Vegas. I'm sure there are still many things I could learn from him. *A Diamond on the Wall* may be purchased at www.createspace.com/3769609 for about nine dollars. It is also available on e-books for less for the Kindle and Nook.

I have known Bradley for ten years. He will be seventeen in September, 2012, and, I love him dearly! This assignment of his was completed in early March, 2012, and the topic was of his choosing.

From the first time I met Brad, I saw an amazing young man, possessing tremendous potential, but whose potential was not being evidenced in his life. While it is not my intent to disparage anyone, Bradley's self-esteem was very low, and little was being done to help him see his worth. I silently watched as his dad interacted with him, and what I witnessed is typical of what we all see and hear today. No matter how hard that young boy tried to please his dad, his efforts never were good enough. Every compliment was followed by a "BUT"!

"That was a good report, BUT!" "You did a nice job on the lawn, BUT!" I could go on, BUT I think you get my drift. The compliment never ended on a positive note; it always had to be followed by some sort of "constructive criticism". Every time I heard the "BUT", I saw Bradley's shoulders sag ever so slightly, and knew that the only thing he heard was what was lacking. The compliment was always lost.

It is important to note, however, that Bradley's dad was raised in a very typical working-class atmosphere. Bradley's grandfather worked three jobs to provide for a family of six children, and his grandmother knew nothing other than housework and her own sort of torture under the burden. Very little thought was given to encouragement and nurturing; either between the parents, or from the parents to the children. These parents, like mine, knew the depression; they knew hardship; they knew what it was to want, so their purpose was to provide. Period! Sadly, for those six children, including Bradley's dad, the provision of establishing self-worth and value was replaced by comments such as, "Why do you think we had you (kids), other than to do the chores?" Bradley's dad was raised in an atmosphere of "BUT'S", so that is all he knew to pass along to his child. There is no blame; only a vicious cycle that is never-ending, unless someone becomes willing to engage in a battle to break that cycle.

At the same time Brad was hearing the "BUTS", he was also being bullied by a number of boys at school. The bullying and taunting began for him in the first grade. The teachers witnessed the events and did nothing. Letters were written to the school administrators, and they did nothing. After one particular incident, the primary bully and Brad were both called into the counselor's office, and both were reprimanded. Bradley was heard telling his tormenter to, "Shut-up", and in so speaking, he was chastised.

It is also important for you to know that Bradley was not willing to engage. All he ever wanted was to be left alone. Furthermore, this is a boy with a very soft and gentle heart; the kind of boy who always wanted to please those around him, but whose actions never seemed to be appreciated by anyone other than his mother.

In my personal interactions with Brad, I tried very hard to affirm his self-worth. The effort expended on my part over the years was negligible, all things considered. We would see each other a few times a week in social settings, and I always tried to take a few minutes to ask about his day, to inquire about what he was up to, and the reports were almost always the same. The kids were picking on him, he couldn't concentrate on his homework, he was doing poorly in school, and his shoulders were sagging. His shoulders were always sagging!

With his mom's permission, I began talking with Brad about the other kids. I wanted to know what they were saying that upset him. I asked about the homework and concentration thing too, and the answers were almost all the same. Simply, without positive input, Bradley was giving-up. He was beaten, and he was demoralized.

It saddened me a great deal to see this kid, who had so much potential, being demoralized, so I began lifting him up! I complimented him, without any "BUT". I encouraged him without reservations. Oh, I got angry with him too, when he'd do something silly, but even then, my verbal discipline was never demoralizing or intentionally hurtful. If discipline was in order, I addressed the issue, not the person. "This was wrong", Not, "You were wrong". Whenever he did something right, he received a compliment. Whenever he did something wrong, we talked about the wrong, with respect – and love! It does not take a Ph.D. to do these things.

While I was encouraging Brad, his mom and Charlie, my wife, were encouraging him too. Sadly though, about five years ago, his mom and dad divorced. I think much of it had to do with the fact that both Bradley and his mom were unable to take the "BUTS" anymore. Personally, I could never explain this to Brad's dad, and I feel sorry for that.

As the encouragement increased in his life though, Bradley began to change. The lad began to show signs of self-confidence and self-worth, and this was especially true during summer break, when the bullies weren't there to taunt him. As soon as school was back in session though, the bullies continued their tormenting, and true to form, the teachers did nothing. They knew who was bullying whom, but they did nothing!

I sat with Brad after he returned from school on one particularly bad day, in which the primary bully in his life actually began poking him in the stomach, calling him names. And that was when I had had enough. We contacted the school administrators and advised them what was happening. We spoke with the teachers, who saw the events unfold, but again, they did nothing. So, I advised Bradley what to do.

In our chat I told Brad that if he wanted this kid to finally stop bullying him, he had to be willing to engage. Instead of pleading with him to 'stop', he was going to have to engage. "By engaging him in this way," I said, "you will put an end to your torment". I warned Brad though, and his mom too, that if he did what I was advising, he was going to receive some sort of punishment for his actions. But, "do this one time, and this kid will NEVER taunt, bully, or touch you inappropriately again".

My advice was very, very simple (and predictable to you, I am certain):

"Bradley, make a fist as tight as you can, and the next time this bully touches you in any way, in a bullying manner, punch him in the face as hard as you possibly can." And that is precisely what he did.

And the school officials reacted exactly as I predicted.

I wrote to the school administrator and to the school district offices. In my letters I cited dates and times in which we had contacted the school, the teachers and anyone else necessary, in order to enlist their help in shutting down the bully, but they did NOTHING! In my letter I protested Bradley's punishment, but the reply I received was, "This is policy".

Well folks, if it remains school policy to punish kids who are merely defending themselves, from a known bully, when the school authorities are fully aware of EVERYTHING, then school policies need to be changed.

Bradley did as advised, and he received the punishment I knew would be forthcoming. But more importantly, the bully never touched or tormented him again. It took six years to convince this soft-hearted young man to "engage" his bully. Six years of torment – for what?

I am not telling this story merely to talk about Bradley and his very complimentary and humbling essay. I am telling this story, because too many people today are being tormented by bullies, and the fact that we remain unwilling to engage causes our plight to worsen daily.

It does not matter if you are a conservative or a liberal, an optimist or a pessimist, a passive personality or an aggressive personality. Differences between people will always exist. What does matter is that you never surrender who you are as an individual, because someone else is shouting louder than you, or pushing harder than you. You matter! Your opinion matters! And anytime anyone with an opposing opinion shouts you down in order to get their way, and you allow it, you have allowed yourself to be reduced to zero, and I guarantee you – your shoulders will be sagging!

Varying and differing opinions are not necessarily bad things in and of themselves. Backing down, however, because the bully is bigger or louder or more insistent, IS a bad thing. And to be perfectly candid, our nation and world are in trouble today, because people have grown silent through the conditioning of the bullies. Too tired, intimidated, complacent, and unwilling to engage, society has been conditioned to believe they cannot stop the slide. Unless we become willing to engage, in whatever area holds our particular interest or angst, however, matters are only going to get worse.

The bullies are the same today as they've always been; only more sophisticated at times. The bottom line is that a very violent and vocal minority is bullying a very passive, compliant, complacent silent majority, and until they decide to wake up and engage the bullies, matters on a worldwide basis are going to get worse.

Bradley was finally willing to engage, and his primary tormentor backed down.

Today, what with technology being what it is, Bradley is able to play games on his computer, against game playing opponents from around the world, and as these kids play, they talk. And, as they talk, before I moved and during a recent visit, I heard Bradley telling other kids to NOT allow the bullies to get away with it; to stand up for their rights. He even gets very vocal during a game in which he is involved, when one individual tries to bully another person verbally. Bradley simply will not allow it to continue, and will break-off a game with a bully in an instant, if they persist.

My sixteen year old friend has learned to engage, and is encouraging other kids to do the same thing; to not allow the bullies to win; to take a stand for their rights. Needless to say, I am very proud of Bradley.

So, rhetorically speaking, when was the last time you defended yourself when the bully shouted you down? When was the last time you were willing to engage on behalf of your belief, instead of being voted down without casting your ballot? When was the last time you reached out to assist another, when you saw them being bullied? And here is an even harder question:

<u>"Even if your opinion is in agreement with the bully, when was the last time you protected a meeker individual, who simply wanted to voice their opinion (or did you stand by and allow the bully to win)?"</u> **If you stood by and allowed the bully to beat down another individual, then you are just as guilty as the bully.** Think about that!

Being willing to engage does not mean being willing to get physical, although there are times when that is part of it too. Being willing to engage is simply possessing the mindset that you matter; that your opinion matters and that you have the right to express that opinion without being bullied or tormented, and every other person has those same rights.

The fact that we can remain silent no more is necessitated by the reality that a very vocal few are dominating the many, and the voices of those few are being fueled in ways that we simply refuse to acknowledge or see.

I reached out to a young lad in a very simple and positive way, and the results were, and are, magnificent. Bradley walks with his shoulders straight today. Did I do that all by myself? Absolutely not! The plain truth of the matter is that someone began something positive in his life, and enlisted the help of others to continue the positive feedback. And together, we now watch a strong young man getting stronger and stronger every day, and he is helping other kids do the same thing. That is very cool, and that is the reward for being willing to engage.

Did we do anything superhuman? Absolutely not! The bottom line to the reality of this is simply that we cared enough to get involved, and once involved, we then actually stepped-up to the plate. Can you do the same thing? Absolutely you can!

What is it that concerns you? What is it that has your interest? What do you see happening that you would like to see changed? No matter what the concern, interest, or issue, unless you are willing to engage, and actually get involved in seeking a viable and acceptable solution, nothing will change. Without engaging in the battle, nothing will ever change.

Whenever I hear someone bitching that did not even voice their opinion at the polls and vote, I want to scream, "Shut Up!" What they have to say is meaningless, because they didn't care enough to engage. Unless you are willing to engage, and be silent no more, and that includes going to the polls and voting, then you have absolutely NOTHING to say about the issues. By not voting you have reduced yourself to zero, and your complaining is as a puff of cold air. Unless you are willing to speak-up and fight for what you believe, then all you are doing is bitching, and to be honest, no one wants to hear it!

100

Got a concern? Find an organization working toward addressing that concern and get involved. If you cannot find an organization that is working toward solving your concern, start one!

And if you think yourself incapable of starting an organization, begin by writing to the "Letters to the Editor" section of your local newspaper, and express your concern. Perhaps you will stir others who feel the same as you. Somewhere along the way you will find the person (or people) who will know how to get an organization rolling, and together you can all work toward resolving whatever issue it is that you collectively wish to resolve.

Without a willingness to engage, however, and without putting an end to our silence, the bullies will continue their rampage over us, and we will lose.

Truly, we can be silent no more!

(Thomas Jefferson)

"The spirit of resistance to government is so valuable on certain occasions that I wish it to be always kept alive. It will often be exercised when wrong, but better so than not to be exercised at all."

(Richard Posey Campbell)

WHILE THE CEMETERY YAWNS

Old age creeps on with a slow, sure tread
And your hair grows white and thin,
Your eyes get bad and your teeth fall out
And your nose comes down to your chin;
While the little old graveyard on the hill
Seems to beckon as you go past
And your kind friends say as they shake their heads,
"Yes, the old man is failing fast."
But your grave's undug and you're not dead yet,
So let the funeral wait.
Go get you a set of new store teeth
And a wig for your shining pate;
Have your tailor build you a knobby suit
And purchase a flaming tie,
Then jump right into the middle of things
And forget that you'll ever die.
This poor old world's in an awful fix
And is sadly in need of you,
So roll up your sleeves and pitch right in
And sweat like you used to do.
You are worth too much with your wealth of brain
And the grasp of things that is yours,
To go and crawl down into your grave
And play with the roots of flowers.
So hunt up the doctor and pay him off
And take his receipt in full,
Then get down under the load once more
And give it the old time pull.
We need you so, wc can't spare you yet,
A life is too dearly bought.
The world should pluck and winnow with care
Its harvest of ripened thought.

Chapter 8 – So, Where to from Here?

I am always amazed to see how much we can accomplish, when we really want to get something done. Just look at the reaction generated whenever natural disasters occur. The tsunami in Japan in 2011 is a perfect example. The response from around the world was not only immediate, it was massive. Aid poured into that country from all four corners of the globe, and it was wondrous. The same is true of many similar events. We have the capacity to accomplish tremendous feats, whenever we set our hearts upon achieving something. This same truth can be applied to each and every one of us, because we each have the capacity to accomplish magnificent and wondrous things.

Why though, does it take a huge disaster to warrant our attention? If we open our eyes, we can see countless mini-disasters happening all about us every day. And yet, even in the seeing, we remain blind and mute to these mini-disasters; we remain silent. Perhaps we sit and watch because we are overwhelmed by the enormity of it all, or by the fact that there is only so much one person can do. On the other hand, maybe we sit and watch because we feel unqualified to tackle any given task. Whatever the reason, we are silent and uninvolved, when in fact, singly and united, we can accomplish great things, and resolve or eliminate many of those mini-disastrous issues. Singly and collectively, we can make a difference.

Please allow me to provide a few examples of matters that concern me:

➤ In our education system, in spite of the fact that more money is spent per student in the United States, than anywhere else in the world, the actual number of illiterate students (children and adults, who can neither read nor write), is increasing. That is despicable!

Although I believe I know why illiteracy is increasing, I also know there are millions of people in the United States who do know how to read. Those who can read can help teach others, if they want to help, and if we provide the tools needed to accomplish the task. All it would take is a few hours per week, for a united group of willing "activists" across the country to eliminate the illiteracy issue.

We are illiterate, by the way, because we have abandoned the proven method of using phonics for teaching proper reading skills, and have instead adopted whatever whimsical method is in vogue within a corrupt and politically driven Department of Education. We can fix that. If we want our children to read again, we can demand our educators return to using phonics as the sole method for reading instruction, and when we do, the illiteracy problem will be solved. Continue the way we are though, and matters will worsen.

Imagine then, if you will, that instead of it being me sprawled out on the floor of that high school hallway, on the first day of my freshman year; that it is our children and grandchildren who are sprawled out on the floor; their books are splattered about them, and a decision must be made. Are we going to sit on the floor with them, and continue being bullied, and thereby allow an ever increasing number of our children, grandchildren and great-grandchildren to become illiterate, or are we finally going to engage on their behalf?

"We the People" have the authority to tell the Department of Education to return to the strict usage of phonics in the education of our children. Honest, we do! If we unite and become willing to engage in this battle, we have that authority. As a matter of fact, we have the authority to insist that the entire Department of Education be disbanded, IF WE SO CHOOSE. We also have the authority to dictate other matters regarding the education of our children. As other issues are brought to our attention, we can demand that corrections be made. And yet, although a great number of people are striving to correct many of the issues within the Department of Education, they cannot accomplish the task without our help.

104

But here's the thing, currently the vast majority of us are sitting on the floor, right along with our children and grandchildren, and we are allowing a bully to dictate how our children are to be educated, in spite of that bully's proven failures, and in spite of illiteracy, and in spite of all the other educational shortcomings within our current system. The bully insists that "No Student shall be left behind" and those few citizens who are trying to fight on our behalf are simply overwhelmed, because they are fighting against a huge gang of bullies, and they will not succeed unless we intervene. They need us to get off the floor and join the fight. The question is, "Are we Willing To Engage"? Are we willing to be "Silent No More"? Are we finally willing to speak out against what we know is a dismally failing bully?

Here's another example to consider:
➤ According to RAINN (Rape, Abuse and Incest National Network), someone in the United States of America is sexually assaulted every 2 minutes. Furthermore, <u>15 out of every 16 rapists will never spend a day in jail</u>.

Rape is an offense that should be punishable by death. (Check out the Bible, folks). Nonetheless, rapists today receive a slap on the wrist for their offense, and are returned to society within a few years (if they are jailed at all), and once returned to society, they are free to repeat their crime. And, if they are imprisoned, "We the People" pay for their every need.

Think about this, ladies especially, because YOU (more than any other group) to a great degree, are allowing this travesty to happen to yourselves. As far as legitimate voters are concerned, women are in the majority, and yet, even with that distinct voting advantage, you cannot seem to unite enough to put an end to the insanity that currently reigns regarding rape, abuse and/or incest.

If you seriously want to stop these abuses, you must voice your concern, and insist upon the appropriate changes with your local Representatives. If those local Representatives do not react, then locate and vote for Representatives who will take a very strong stand on the issue. Locate and elect Representatives who are willing to pass and enforce extremely strict laws, which will remove the burden from the abused, and place that burden squarely on the criminals. These actions will provide the means to allow our law enforcement agencies to capture those who are now getting away with their crime, and ***severely punish*** *all convicted of incest, rape and abuse.*

Our women and children have been pushed to the floor; their bodies lay violated about us, and a decision must now be made. Are we going to allow our women and children to lay on the floor and be raped or abused, or are we finally going to engage on their behalf?

In context with this line of thought is the fact that child slavery, and the abduction of children and young girls (especially), is occurring at an alarming rate. Many of these children are being sold and moved to foreign countries, where they are enslaved in sex-mills. And, very little is being done to shut down these abuses. Along with protecting our borders against illegal immigration and the illegal entry of drugs, we must also protect our children from being shipped out of this country for use as sex slaves.

If we unite, and if we are willing to engage in the battle against rape, abuse, abduction and incest; then rape, abuse, abduction and incest will become minor issues.

Let's not forget the basic premise from which I am laboring though, because if you do not agree with at least a portion of my basic premise, we are not speaking the same language. Primarily, I believe that each person has tremendous value and worth. Every person has worth! Every person has value! Every person alive is unique and precious! Therefore, each of us is worth fighting for, and it does not matter where you sit politically when it comes to these issues, because matters of personal respect transcend political lines. We either believe that fact or we do not.

Personally, I have never met a man, woman or child deserving of sexual abuse! Have you? Personally, I cannot envision any individual deserving treatment as a slave, let alone as a sex-slave! Have you? Personally, I cringe at the thought of incest and rape, and stand in horror in the light of the abuses "We the People" are permitting within our country, and within our world.

So then, if these matters disturb you at all, I challenge you to become engaged. I challenge you to speak up, and do something. I challenge you to join with others who are trying to put an end to this insanity, because they need our help. Are you willing to help? Are you Willing To Engage? Are you willing to be Silent No More?

Want more? Here is another example:

➢ On a worldwide basis, drug abuse is another area of tremendous waste, and it is an issue that we must face head on. I read a quote recently at the abovetheinfluence.com website that really touched me. In its simplicity it said, "With so many voices and opinions out there, sometimes all you need is the knowledge to make your own decisions."

I could not agree more, because being willing to engage requires that we be knowledgeable in whatever area we choose to become involved.

The simple truth of the drug abuse issue lies in the fact that we are allowing this to happen. If you want to stop drug abuse, shut down the drug producers. If you want to stop the flow of drugs into the United States of America, or any other country, then seriously shut down the borders and inlets of the nation. And then go after the people, who are making the illicit drugs; who are trying to import those drugs into the country.

One obvious solution (to me) comes to mind, and while I am certain other men and women are laboring to solve the problem, I offer the following simply for your consideration:

The "cold war" in Europe is over. In spite of that fact, "We the People" of the United States of America, are still paying the bill to station tens of thousands of U.S. troops in Europe, to fight against an enemy that no longer exists. Why?

Instead of pumping our money into Europe, defending nothing, bring our troops home, and position them along our borders, to actually defend The United States of America. In the process, we not only labor toward shutting down the illegal entry of drugs and people into (and out of) this country, but we bolster our own economy in the process.

This is a win-win scenario folks. Finances aside, by bringing our soldiers and sailors home from Europe, we can position them, and our military might, along our borders (land and sea), and in the process shut down the illegal flow of drugs and people into this country, as well as shut down the illegal flow of abducted women and children going out of this country.

According to the Department of Defense, two massive Divisions are about to be pulled out of Germany and be dismantled. Why are we dismantling these units, when we need their protection here at home?

> Another step in the battle against drug abuse (and is this ever radical), is to drug screen every welfare and food-stamp recipient within the country, and deny financial aid to anyone who fails that drug screening. This is not a new idea, but this certainly is a common sense approach to a number of appalling abuses.

"We the People" are in debt, because we have allowed special interest groups to influence every aspect of our lives. We have been pushed to the floor by the bullies, and we either become willing to engage in battle against those bullies, or we will find ourselves living in a Socialistic Society, instead of a Free Republic! The decision to engage must happen NOW though, because five more years of the idiocy we see displayed today, and the nation of the United States of America will be in ruin. That is a prophetic message!

"We the People" must be willing to engage in an intense battle for our nation and people, and in that engagement we must fight for the return to the intent of the Constitution of this Republic. We must also reapply the intent of our legal system in the process.

My original goal for this chapter was to reveal some of the little ways in which we could become engaged in our society today. But in all reality, anything we do, everything we do, on an individual or group basis, in any effort to help any other person within our society, is a good thing.

We can help children and adults learn to read, and empower those children and adults in the process.

We can help children and adults who have been victims of rape, incest or abuse by punishing the offenders, and by making anyone even considering such a heinous act to think twice, because the punishment for such an offense is life-ending.

We can initiate work programs for those drug-free recipients of welfare aid and food stamps, and give them self-worth and pride, instead of a free handout. In the process we can rebuild the infrastructure of our nation. In so doing, we will also cure some of our financial ills as well.

Chain-gang labor for those imprisoned for crimes against society is not an outrageous thought either. Criminals need to pay for their keep. The free handout must come to an end.

We can correct the abuses to our Social Security and Medicare programs, and provide the aid needed by those who actually paid for these things. Instead of throwing these monies at illegal immigrants, who are merely taking whatever the radical and vocal minority is giving away today, "We the People" can repair these ills. Social Security and Medicare ARE NOT ENTITLEMENTS. Check your paystub, folks. You (and your employer) are, and have been, paying for these INSURANCES. Those who have not paid do not deserve to participate. Certainly not at the level in which they participate today!

We can visit the sick and the elderly, and reaffirm their value and worth, even if those visits merely convey a kind word, or a listening ear.

We can be respectful toward the people we meet, and in every meeting we have, with anyone, we can positively make a difference in that person's day and life.

We can stop the bullies in the schools – and I do mean shut them down. We can take an absolute non-abuse stand against those who are making life miserable for their fellow students. We can hold administrators, teachers and school board officials accountable when our non-abuse position is violated. In the process, we can help find kids who are thinking about suicide, because of the abuses they are suffering, and extend a helping hand. By shutting down the bullies we can reaffirm the self-worth of those who have been abused in the process. But doing nothing is no longer an option.

All we need to do in order to accomplish any and all of these tasks, is to become willing to engage. We can remain silent and complacent no more, because if we do, we will lose that which we have grown complacent about! We are needed in every battle being fought for sanity, and the only way those already engaged in the fight can win, is if we, the silent majority, join in their engagement.

I am striving to do my part through the telling of a story I would rather not share, as well as through the ministry we have had in place for the last twenty-four years at The Letters of Faith website. Furthermore, I am willing to redouble my effort whenever and wherever I can, in order to engage against the tyrants and the bullies.

The question that must be answered though is:

How "Willing To Engage" are YOU?

Chapter 9 – Coming Full Circle

For twenty-four years I have used my "Letters of Faith" website as a platform to share lessons regarding the Bible, and how the very Word of God should impact our lives on a day-by-day basis. From the outset of those lessons though, I make a promise to my visitors that no matter what the overall topic of any particular letter might be, in response to whatever questions were being asked at that time, somewhere within each letter; personal self-worth, the tremendous value of each individual, respect, or God's love, will somehow be emphasized. It wasn't until this very moment though, I realized how closely the emphasis of those issues emanates from the first philosophical lesson I ever learned, or how thoroughly The Letters of Faith, which are based upon the very Word of God, reflect my childhood lessons.

As I consider everything I have ever written, shared, or spoken, somewhere within my message, the fullness of our uniqueness, value, and personal self-worth can be found.

And finally, in regard to these matters, little did I know when I began writing this prequel to "A Diamond on The Wall", that the lessons I learned in my childhood, and which remained deeply ingrained in my heart throughout my tumultuous years, were going to permeate these pages.

I recently received a packet from friends in Medford, which contained copies of notes I had inadvertently left behind in my snow-bird move to Nevada. They were concerned I might need those notes for this book. The notes, strangely enough, were written five years ago, and as I read through those pages, I was stunned to see the beginning stages of a variation of THIS book. The notes were presented in a different format of course, which did not include my tumultuous years, yet the overall message contained within those notes offers the same encouragement and motivation I am attempting to provide here. It appears to me, through all of this, that my heart and mind are singularly focused upon establishing within you, the deep-seated fullness of the fact that we each have tremendous value and self-worth; that the coin we possess (the gift, talent or ability that we have each been given), is unique and priceless, and purposeful. And, that if we do not use that coin, we devalue that which is fully intended to be of substantial worth to the whole of mankind.

Clearly, helping to establish your self-worth, value, and uniqueness, is wrapped up entirely within the use of my personal coin, and if I do not press on in this endeavor, I will in fact be burying my own coin, which is something I simply am unable or unwilling to do. As I have said repeatedly throughout my writings, "I never knew how to back down (or give up), so I plowed through".

Within the pages I just received, I found the definitions of two words that I think are connected to this discussion. Those two words are: Enable and Disable, and I offer "Webster's" definition of both words here for your consideration:

➢ ENABLE: To make able; authorize or empower. To make possible or easy. ENABLING: conferring legal power or sanction, as by removing a disability!

> "As by removing a disability"! Think about that for a moment, will you?

➢ DISABLE: To make unable or unfit; weaken or destroy the capability of; cripple. To make legally incapable; disqualify.

> "To weaken or destroy the capability of"!

When people speak about the endurable nature of the human spirit, it seems to me that more often than not we are marveling a bit at the accomplishments of others. Usually, we shrug our shoulders as we marvel, but we do not seem to realize that we each have the capacity to enable another soul to endure – and ultimately to succeed. Through a kind word, through a simple act or deed, or merely through coming alongside someone we see struggling, whether we say anything or not, is an enabling act, which may just help that person succeed.

Our silence, or our lack of involvement, may very well weaken or destroy the capability of someone who is actually willing to engage, on our behalf. Organizations exist today which are attempting to correct many of the ills of society, but for those people to succeed in their endeavor, they need our help, encouragement, support, voice, and perhaps, even our vote. Following the Epilogue of this book, I am providing a list of any number of organizations involved in any number of battles, and I challenge you to read the list, and examine your heart, to see if you cannot locate a group that is already fighting in an area of personal interest to you, but who may be in need of your assistance; who may be in need of your voice. And, when/if you locate that group, or groups, I also challenge you to get involved and use your voice and participate. Use your coin!

Not long ago I found myself in the role of an assistant coach for a little league baseball team. Standing out on the field working with those kids reminded me of the joy I experienced, so many years ago, when I coached my elementary school basketball team. And the new experience transformed me in many ways.

I was dismayed, however, by the parents who believed that their child should catch every ball, or get a hit every time they came to the plate. And the conversations that ensued on the sidelines between innings were a source of tremendous harm to many of those kids, because all too often, the words were harsh, biting and disabling.

We each have the capacity to uphold, uplift, authorize and empower, and just as easily as we can simplify a task, encourage an individual, or remove a disability, we also have the capacity to weaken, destroy and disqualify a person. We can choose the route we are going to take; we can choose to enable, or we can choose to disable.

In 1911, Ty Cobb, notably the best baseball hitter/batter of all time, hit the ball 42% of the time he went to bat. The following year his average slipped to 40.9%. In a brilliant 24-year career, Ty Cobb averaged to hit the ball 36.6% of the time. (That is just slightly better than one hit every three times at bat). The best of the best, in the history of baseball, hit the ball 36.6% of the time, yet many parents today expect their children to accomplish feats that they themselves, let alone the best of the best, are incapable of accomplishing; they actually expect their children to get a hit every time they step up to the plate. And for what, pride?

Well, where is pride to be found if we destroy the value and self-worth of our children, our mates, our parents, or anyone else for that matter, if we belittle and denigrate that person, because they are incapable of meeting our outrageous and unattainable expectations?

Where is pride to be seen if we sit and silently enable a vocal minority to alter the course of history, and destroy a nation for which countless hundreds of thousands have died to establish and uphold? Within the pages of this book I have quoted two of the most remarkable documents ever written by mankind: The Declaration of Independence and The First Ten Amendments to the Constitution of the United States, better known as The Bill of Rights, so that you can take a moment to read and understand precisely what it is that those countless hundreds of thousands have died to defend. My hope is that in reading these documents, you will find the motivation to take a stand, to use your coin, and engage to in the battle for life, liberty and freedom.

Where is pride if we remain silent and uninvolved, if we permit the bullies to taunt and diminish the value of another individual; to devalue life itself? And this particular battle truly must include our silence in regard to the issue of abortion, because the unborn have no voice, only silent and unheard screams as their lives, and lifeblood, are drained and thrown away as yesterday's garbage. With the support of our government, and that would be, "We the People", since the Roe-v-Wade decision altered the course and value of life, and allowed abortion on demand, which of the sixty million children aborted, in the United States alone, might have been the doctor or scientist who would have discovered the cure for cancer? Which of those sixty million aborted babies might have been the leader capable of negotiating peace in the Middle East? Which of those slaughtered sixty million infants might have invented pure and renewable energy? The list of possible accomplishments that might have been attained by those sixty million boys and girls is endless, and yet many of us remain silent as the slaughter continues.

Where is pride to be found today, if we refuse to engage on behalf of whatever it is that we deem to be of value, and allow that person, place or thing of value to be destroyed through our silence? And precisely what is it going to take to make the silent majority rise up, engage in the battles, and be silent no more?

Sadly too, as this book and my story have shown, the effort required to make a difference is not huge. Not really! This is especially true when there are so many of us who can offer small bits of assistance, which collectively amount to massive amounts of help. All it would have taken is for two or three teachers to stand beside me in my battles with the school administrators, as I attempted to defend myself, and the true bullies could have been shut down. Where is the pride then, when we choose to ignore the plight of others, or worse, when we choose to exploit the weaknesses of those fighting for their existence, instead of fortifying and uplifting those who find themselves in a weakened and/or defenseless state?

To my younger readers, I encourage you to stop the bullies in your schools. I encourage you to engage in unity against a bully, whenever you see another student being taunted. Together, we can put an end to bullying, but we must want to end that behavior; we must want to stop the torment we witness every day. Whether you believe this today or not, the simple fact of the matter is that every individual has the potential to change the world! Right or wrong, good or bad, the potential exists within each of us to alter the path of the lives of those around us, and possibly, through our interactions with those people, alter the path of humankind.

The power of sincere encouragement, or the impact of derogatory criticism, can so influence a fragile soul, that the entire path of that soul's life can be impacted, either for good, or for harm. And we each have the power to either offer that encouragement or criticism, every day of our lives. I challenge you to uplift, encourage and uphold those around you. I challenge you to use your coin. I assure you, in the process of doing these things – your shoulders will never again sag!

Try it folks: Go ahead and offer that smile, hold open that door, nod in acknowledgement, feel free to applaud the successes as well as the failed attempts of others. After all, isn't it true that expending the effort to accomplish something is equally important, whether the goal was actually met or not? Success comes through the practice and the trying, and every sincere effort should be acknowledged equally. Be willing to engage, even if you fail the first few times, because eventually, you may be the biggest winner of all! Don't give up or surrender, just plow through!

And in my own way of plowing through, I am willing to engage on the side of uplifting, upholding, and encouraging. But, it must be noted that as I endeavor to engage in these things, those qualities are not administered without fair and proper discipline. Much of the difficulty we see taking place in the world today in the lives of our youth, has been brought about because too many people are afraid to engage when discipline is required; afraid to engage in the proper instruction demanded when an error is witnessed.

If we are willing to engage properly, and discipline appropriately for the wrong act, instead of disciplining in anger against the person, we will discover an entirely receptive generation awaiting our properly motivated corrections.

Being Willing To Engage, and remaining Silent No More, is about overcoming our personal fears and weaknesses, as we unite in an effort to correct the errors that we have made, or have allowed to be made, and to accomplish these things positively and respectfully, for the betterment of all mankind. We have the capacity to change the world.

How willing are you to engage in that endeavor?

Chapter 10 – Stress & Life 101

Perhaps the greatest response I hear today, in regard as to why people do NOT get involved in matters that require, or actually demand, our attention is, "Life is stressful enough as it is, and I am too busy to really devote the time and attention needed to do what might be required!"

Please permit me to tell you one last story from my childhood; because within this story you will discover the response I am forced to offer whenever I hear that excuse: I was eight years old, and we were still living in the house behind the delicatessen, when I awoke at about midnight one summer night, needing to use to the bathroom. When I woke, I walked into the kitchen, and as I was about to turn left toward the bathroom, I heard noises coming from the front of the house, or from the store, so I walked into the living room to see what was causing the noise. Primarily I was looking to see if anyone had broken into the store. I stopped well short of going out into the store though, because the noise was coming from my parents' bedroom, and what I witnessed is something I have never forgotten.

Mom and dad slept on separate single beds, and those beds were arranged at ninety degree angles from each other. Looking toward the noise, I saw my mom, sitting at the foot of her bed, and dad sitting at the foot of his bed, and they were holding hands, while dad sat – crying!

Through his tears, my dad was saying he just did not know how they were going to pay all of the bills that were due that month. The pressure he was feeling; the stress he was enduring, led my dad to cry in utter despair. As he sobbed, mom tried to console him, but his tears welled-up from the depth of his heart. I watched for only a moment, as my dad's gut-wrenching sense of hopelessness literally caused his body to shake.

I had never seen this side of my dad before, and with tears in my own eyes, I quietly turned and headed back to the bathroom. Once done, I returned to bed, where I prayed for my mom and dad, before finally falling asleep.

The next morning, when I awoke, I went out into the deli and watched my dad as he interacted with the customers throughout the day. I quietly did my chores, and elected to remain near my dad as the day progressed, instead of going out to play. Throughout the day I saw dad greet every customer with his usual, very sincere smile, and customary welcome. To my amazement, I watched as my dad continued to extend credit to people who he and mom knew were substantially behind in making payments on what they already owed. And he did this, knowing that without helping those folks, many of them, and their children, would have gone without food.

In spite of the extent of their own indebtedness, my parents continued to allow their customers to purchase on credit, because they knew those people were worse off financially than they. In spite of the stress over paying their massive debts, most of which were medical bills, my dad continued to dig an even deeper financial hole, and I was stunned beyond expression, as he joyously went through his workday, reached deep into his heart, and shared everything he had within, and without! This is another reason I loved my dad as deeply as I did!

I never said a word about what they were doing, nor did I ever ask, "Why?" I witnessed the response to any questions I might have had every day through their actions, and I have never forgotten what I witnessed. By not forgetting these things, I have been able to live my life with a depth of understanding which allows me, I believe, to write this sort of missive.

No matter how deep the hole became, and no matter how much stress they felt because of their financial burden and health issues, my parents continued to operate under the belief that somehow, money would come from somewhere, and they would be caught up with their bills. As I have already mentioned, money always did come at the exact time it was needed the most, from unusual places, to say the least. When it did come, the bills were brought up to date or paid-off, and we ate Chinese!

While I never saw my dad cry again over money, I never forgot that night, and I was aware of the financial pinch that gripped them both. In that knowledge, I always prayed that they would have enough money to pay the bills, and live with their needs met.

The knowledge of these things, therefore, and my continued prayers on their behalf throughout my tour of duty in Vietnam, explains why I was not tremendously upset when I learned that the money I had sent home was used to sustain them. How could I be angry about the manner in which my Father in Heaven provided for my parents?

Yes, I was disappointed they never told me what was happening, as if they didn't trust me. But I was never really angry about the money itself. Father had provided for their needs in answer to my very own prayers, so being angry would have been hypocritical.

And here is where I am forced to draw a line in the sand with regard to anyone saying they are too stressed, too busy, or too, whatever, to get involved in the matters taking place before us today, knowing that if we remain silent; knowing that if we refuse to engage in the battle confronting us, that matters will most certainly get worse; then we are, in fact, being hypocritical!

If I were to offer a lesson entitled, "Life 101", I would probably begin the first lesson by saying, "90% of the time, we choose our stressors". It's true! We frequently choose that which we allow to cause us stress. "Furthermore", I would add, "not only do we choose most of our stressors, but, if we get involved in solving those stressful matters, instead of running from them, as the silent majority is doing today, we could eliminate most of the issues causing our stress!"

Being willing to engage transcends whether we "feel up to doing something or not", just as much as overcoming fear transcends the need for a soldier to react effectively, positively and as forcibly as necessary, in times of battle. It's really not about fear; it's what you do with fear that matters.

The silent majority has been pushed to the floor by the bullies, and unless we engage those bullies now, we will subject ourselves to the most frightening lifestyle changes imaginable. The key words within that statement are, "ENGAGE NOW"! It may already be too late. We may already be out of time. We may have remained docile too long. Surely, we have allowed a very vocal minority of radical extremists to run roughshod over our Constitution, our country, and our world, and this "Call to Arms" may very well be the last of its sort, from a common, non-political citizen, because as our freedoms are lost, I assure you, the freedom of speech will be among the first to go. That is, after they remove our second amendment right to bear arms!

Matters of immense significance are out of whack today, and unless we immediately do what is needed to set them straight right now, we may never have another opportunity. Another five years of the idiocy we see coming from the leaders of our nation and world today, our world will be so outrageously transformed, there will be no recovery.

Continuing in my "Life 101" lesson mode then, I would have to offer the truth that power is a force that can be used for good or evil, and that when undisciplined people are given any sort of power or authority, in all probability, those undisciplined individuals will use that power in evil, destructive and undisciplined ways. This is true, because undisciplined power and authority always seeks immediate gratification and reward, while disciplined power and authority always labor toward long-term and long-lasting positive results.

Sadly, in the democracy of this Republic, a very vocal minority of truly undisciplined bullies is giving away the store, buying the vote in the process, while a very docile and silent majority refuses to engage and stop the idiocy. Let me ask you something, and this comes from the depth of the lessons I learned as I watched my parents work their way out of debt: "How are integrity, respect and

120

responsibility supposed to be learned, when nothing is expected in return for the handouts provided by our current government?"

Specifically, here are a few items that irritate me a great deal. I wonder, at times, if these matters annoy others too. I'm offering my idea of solutions as well. What do you think?

> Our government is giving away billions of dollars every year to people who are in this country **illegally**, whether that money is issued in the form of welfare, food stamps, free education, Pell Grants, etc. These indulgences include the imprisonment, and provision of all needs, of thousands of illegal immigrants who have committed crimes against the citizens of this nation. While this is taking place, the elderly and truly needy citizens of the United States are living below poverty levels.

"We the People" are allowing this to happen, and the situation worsens every year. When are we going to do something about the iniquity of these matters? I believe we need to do the following:

- Immediately halt the illegal flow of people into this country. (And end the exporting of kidnapped citizens going out). And immediately return all illegal immigrants back to their home countries.
- Immediately halt the illegal flow of drugs into this country.
- We must execute all criminals convicted of heinous crimes (Murder, rape, and kidnapping would be a good start).
- Immediately reform of our prison system, and return all other convicted illegal immigrants BACK to their home countries. These criminals are here illegally. "We the People" are not responsible for maintaining them.

In the return of illegal immigrant criminals back to their home country though, their return must be accompanied with a warning, that if they ever return to the United States illegally again, their recapture (and we will recapture them), will be cause for more extreme measures.

"Back in the day", people were hung for stealing a horse or cattle. Today, we permit mass murderers and rapists to walk freely amongst us. When did "We the People" stop demanding true justice for crimes committed?

I am told that my position on execution stands in conflict with my position on upholding the value and self-worth of the individual, and that I am being hypocritical in speaking out against illegal immigration, because, after all, illegal immigrants only want a better life. In response, I can only say that the hypocrisy lies in the fact that we are allowing greater liberty and benefit to those who are within our boundaries illegally, than we are providing our own citizens. By permitting those guilty of heinous crimes to "get away with their criminal deeds", we are encouraging others to attempt the same heinous acts, thereby multiplying those offenses. Our first priority must be for the care and protection of our citizens; this is true of any country.

➢ Our government is giving away billions of dollars every year to people who choose to remain on welfare rolls, without requiring anything in return. We do not impose any <u>serious</u> restrictions on how those billions of dollars can, or cannot, be spent. Why?

Because "We the People" are allowing this to happen, the situation worsens every year. When are we going to impose restrictions on these abuses and offer real hope to people who truly do want to improve their life-style; who want to live with integrity; who want to act responsibly; who want to earn the respect that is due all mankind?

- Recipients of welfare and food stamps must be made to pass monthly drug screening (and this screening must include all people living in their home). Failure to pass from anyone abiding within a residence is proof that our tax dollars are providing drug money to the users, and we are not responsible for providing illicit drugs to our welfare recipients.

- Recipients of welfare and food stamps must be given work assignments in order to "earn their keep". Those work assignments must be directed toward the upkeep and maintenance of our cities and national infrastructure.

  (Naturally, these work assignments must also take physical disabilities and age into consideration, but we have work that needs to be done, and these citizens, who are being "paid an income", must be made to contribute to society, and earn that income).

➤ Our government pays billions of dollars every year to provide for the maintenance and upkeep of convicted felons, and expects nothing in return from those within our prison system. Through our silence, "We the People" have allowed this to happen. We can solve this problem though.

- "Work gangs" or "Chain gangs" are not illegal, but for whatever reason, the states stopped using prison inmates for productive purposes decades ago (except Arizona). The expense of prisoner maintenance is now passed on to the citizens of the United States. Supervised, humane, labor, by prison inmates, is an option still available to "We the People", if we so choose. We can mandate a return to work systems within our prisons, and require that all prison inmates, whenever feasible, pay for their upkeep and maintenance. We can also mandate that personal assets be confiscated from convicted felons, when it is within their means to pay their own maintenance and upkeep. We have allowed things to slide to a point which is now entirely out of whack with the needs of OUR nation, however, and we must repair the iniquities of our system. We have elderly and disabled citizens who are living below poverty levels, while convicted felons, imprisoned within our penal system, receive their every need provided for free.

How moronic is this? When are we going to do something about it?

➢ Our government gives away billions of dollars to nations and governments, who literally hate everything we stand for, while we continually turn very slowly away from those nations who have been our allies for decades? Adding insult to injury though, is the fact that at least 42% of those billions of dollars – are now borrowed!

"We the People" are allowing this to happen, and here too, the situation worsens every year. <u>Why are we sending billions of dollars to our enemies, while many of our very own citizens are starving, homeless, and in need of aid?</u> Furthermore, can anyone explain to me how we can send these billions of dollars out in foreign aid, when those dollars are being borrowed from other nations?

I am issuing a warning to the people of the United States of America right now: IF WE EVER TURN OUR BACK ON THE NATION OF ISRAEL, every blessing we have ever known, will be removed! I promised to not be overly zealous on the spiritual side of things, and I believe I have maintained that promise. This particular warning, however, is so very basic and pervasive within the Prophetic portions of Scripture, that to ignore the warnings would be a fatal mistake, which we can ill afford to make!

➢ Our government is spending trillions of borrowed dollars to bailout our economy, all in the wrong areas, and we can't seem to grasp the realities behind the mess the current administration is making. The economic bailout tactic in use today is NOT going to stimulate anything other than temporary jobs, created in the repair of our infrastructure.

Adding insult to injury though, our federal and state governments are actually hiring Chinese corporations, who are employing Chinese laborers, brought in on work visa's, to accomplish the repair and maintenance of many of these, "<u>Putting America Back To Work</u>" bridge and roadway repairs.

Are we really that stupid?

In addition to this insanity, we must realize that the planned projects within healthcare and education are doomed to fail as well. We cannot even teach students how to read properly, so expanding the waste already taking place within the Department of Education will never stimulate anything, and the healthcare package, as discussed, is a debacle in the making.

New growth in our economy will come about when "We the People" understand that local, state and federal regulations have combined to completely choke out new manufacturing. Many manufacturers simply cannot afford to function within our borders any longer. Once we repair our regulatory systems, and once we provide economic stimulus to generate more products to be, "Made in America", we will see the creation of manufacturing jobs throughout the nation.

- We need to eliminate barriers to manufacturing, and enforce barriers for unfair foreign competition. (And this includes the fact we must repeal NAFTA, CAFTA, WTO, GATT, and every other unfair trade agreement which our un-American politicians slipped past a sleeping nation).
- We do not need to eliminate corporate taxes, to our detriment and harm, but we do need to establish fair, reasonable and equitable corporate income taxes, like a flat tax at 25% maximum, thereby allowing corporate and shareholder profits. In so doing, we will discover that those profits will in turn end up back in our own economy!
- We need an intelligent energy plan, which utilizes the proven oil reserves known to exist within our country, and eliminate our dependency on foreign oil completely.

In the process of using our proven resources, we need to eliminate our national and state debts. Coinciding with this is the fact that we need a balanced budget amendment (to the Constitution), which will force our federal government to ABIDE WITHIN OUR means. This is also true for each State.

As we eliminate our debt, and the interest we are currently paying on that debt, we need to invest in the research for alternative energy sources, such as: Solar, Wind and Oceanic Tidal Energy, (as well as whatever else might be dreamt up by those so gifted).

[In any conversation about our national debt though, we must also DEMAND that all monies "borrowed" from the Social Security and Medicare Funds, be repaid – with interest. The national debt today, for which we are in fact paying interest, does not include these stolen monies, but we must mandate the correction of the unconscionable theft from our retirement and medical care insurance funds. "We the People" paid for these insurances, but because of horrible mismanagement by an entitlement driven political machine, our systems, and our citizens are now suffering.]

I could easily add to the above list of issues, which I believe demand our attention, but I believe these points provide ample fuel for consideration with regard to where we are headed as a nation. Unless we become willing to engage and force the bullies to get out of our way, Socialism and Totalitarianism loom on our horizon. We truly cannot be silent any longer, because our continued silence is going to bring about the destruction of our country.

The bottom line is that we have been pushed to the floor, and the bullies are standing cross armed over us, smirking as we silently sit at their feet. The question you must answer is the very same question that raced through my mind on the first day of the ninth grade, as I sat on the floor.

In a retrospective thought of that day, in chapter 6, I said, *"I could easily have remained on the floor that first day of high school, and not struck back. I chose instead to engage and defend. Perhaps through being docile I could have saved myself a tremendous amount of grief, aggravation, pain and suffering; and possibly even have saved my family as well. **But then too, in remaining docile, how susceptible might I have been to other forms of bullying and verbal abuse, because I was deemed a milquetoast or sissy?"***

And that, my friends, is precisely where we are today, because at some point in time, we decided to remain on the floor and allow the bullies to dominate our lives. In allowing that domination, they did precisely as I instinctively knew they would.

I chose to engage and defend back then, and I am choosing to engage and defend once again. I will not permit the bully to stand over me in a position of immature, unrighteous, and undisciplined power and authority, while I still have the freedom and liberty to do something about it. I refuse to surrender my liberties and freedoms without a whimper. But here's the thing: we need Pinky, and Ron I, and Ron II, and Connie, and all the rest the silent majority, and right thinking people, to come alongside, and willingly engage in a united effort, because not one of us can do this alone.

(Thomas Jefferson)

"The two enemies of the people are criminals and government, so let us tie the second down with the chains of the Constitution so the second will not become the legalized version of the first."

(Thomas Jefferson)

"I think myself that we have more machinery of government than is necessary, too many parasites living on the labor of the industrious."

(George Washington)

"Firearms are second only to the Constitution in importance; they are the peoples' liberty's teeth."

Chapter 11 - Politics 101

When looking at the political challenges of our day, I cannot move my mind away from the myriad of idiotic things that we, in the United States of America, are doing on a daily basis; things which are individually and collectively ruinous. Every thought of every malady suffered by our society, ends somewhere in the political heap of garbage that "We the People" have allowed in the name of liberalism, entitlement, elitism, or whatever else you might choose to call it.

In all honesty, much of our difficulties are in fact "spiritual" in nature, but I have promised to not allow my zeal in that arena to impact these writings, and I am striving to abide by that promise.

Nonetheless, almost every country in the world is in serious financial despair, and an honest analysis would reveal that unless managed properly by all involved, a complete, worldwide, financial collapse looms on the horizon. The depression of the 1920's will appear like a sweet dream in comparison to what may very well happen in our day and age, unless "We the People" speak up and engage now.

In times past, things like integrity, fairness, common sense, morality, and knowing, and applying, the difference between right and wrong, was a common bond between people, regardless of which side of any fence or aisle they may have been perched. Today, however, that is no longer true.

A perfect example of zero integrity was revealed when a female Republican Vice-Presidential candidate was slaughtered by a very biased and bigoted full court media press, during the last Presidential election process. The mindless sheep of an "entitlement oriented" people fell right in line though, and watched as that lamb was slaughtered. Sarah Palin may not be a perfect individual. Sarah Palin has certainly made some political and social gaffs, but all-in-all, I will take Sarah Palin's <u>record of accomplishments</u> and compare those accomplishments against everything attained by our current president. I will also make those same comparisons against every other individual running for the Presidential nomination within the Republican Party today.

This same statement, in relationship to the political slaughter of a candidate by a biased media, can also be made regarding one Mr. Alan Keyes:

The black community and the Republican Party, unanimously rejected Alan Keyes as a Presidential candidate. In his campaign, Mr. Keyes spoke the truth to the country, denouncing the entitlement mentality, and promised to initiate the changes needed to salvage our country and economy. Although he is absolutely brilliant, his reasoning and common sense processes are astonishing, and his style and manner of debate overwhelmingly annihilate his opponents, this man's voice fell on deaf ears, and his rejection, as well as Sarah Palin's rejection, is proof that the silent majority was neither willing to engage, nor listen!

John McCain chose a running mate that was too much of a luminary, and instead of stepping back and allowing the tiger they had on their team to run loose – and to appeal to the public, who clearly loved her, He completely mishandled her, exposing her to one of the most biased and prejudicial public assassinations in recent memory, and in the process, lost an election to the most unqualified and incompetent president ever elected.

And if you think my analysis of Ms. Palin's qualifications is overrated, all you need do is watch the continued onslaught being levied against her today, in 2012, by the Hollywood elite. The idiotic movies and caricatures outpouring against her today, continue the "Conditioning" onslaught that was begun 4 years ago. And the intensity of that onslaught, surrounding an unannounced candidate, should tell you that Ms. Palin scares the liberal left today, more than any other potential candidate! The media has so tainted her qualifications in the eyes of the masses though, that she is not even mentioned or seen anywhere on the Republican Party's ticket plans for the upcoming election. Perhaps the most capable "Get-it-done" individual on the scene today has been removed as a challenger, through the conditioning efforts of a biased media. And while that attack is raging, that same media and Hollywood elite are blindly and unquestioningly uplifting their incompetent "god of the moment".

Adding insult to injury, the folks responsible for awarding the Nobel Peace Prize have given what used to be a very prestigious award, to two individuals in recent years, which are entirely out of character for that once reputable philanthropic organization:

- According to the official statement, citing the first such award, "The Nobel Peace Prize 2007 was awarded jointly to Intergovernmental Panel on Climate Change (IPCC) and Albert Arnold (Al) Gore Jr. *'for their efforts to build up and disseminate greater knowledge about man-made climate change, and to lay the foundations for the measures that are needed to counteract such change'*".

While there is little doubt that humanity has caused climactic changes on our planet, by and through our actions, the extent of our impact upon the climate of this planet pale significantly in comparison to the impact of solar activity. The **Maunder Minimum** (also known as the prolonged sunspot minimum) is the name used for the period roughly spanning 1645 to 1715, when sunspots became exceedingly rare, as noted by solar observers of the time. The impact of that solar period of inactivity is known as, "The Little Ice Age."

The current solar cycle is having an opposite impact on our planet today, and the climactic warming we are experiencing is primarily the result of that solar activity. Do we need to alter the way we manage our planet and resources? Absolutely! Do we need to *PANIC* in our rush to change everything we do? Absolutely NOT! We are being conditioned again, however, to believe a great deal of nonsense, and the entire "green" crusade is merely a small part of that conditioning.

- According to the statement awarding the second undeserved award, "The Nobel Peace Prize 2009 was awarded to Barack H. Obama *'for his extraordinary efforts to strengthen international diplomacy and cooperation between peoples'*".

Aside from being elected to the presidency of the United States of America, can anyone actually define what it was that Mr. Obama had done, "To strengthen international diplomacy and cooperation between peoples"? And the conditioning continues…

So how did we arrive at this point?

Let me begin answering that question by getting something straight: When was the last time you met anyone who knew everything about every topic? Never? Yeah, me either! Well then, if that is true, <u>why do we expect our Presidential or Vice-Presidential candidates to have every answer to every question?</u> Why do we have advisors and "Cabinets", if we know everything?

There was a man named Cyrus Eaton, who at one point in his life was one of the top ten richest men in the world. Cyrus Eaton died in 1979 at the age of 95. During his life, although misunderstood at times, Mr. Eaton labored feverishly on behalf of détente and peace throughout the Cold War, as well as the war in Vietnam. Although born in Canada, Cyrus Eaton lived in Cleveland, Ohio.

As a Cleveland native, I once chose to complete a report on the life and labors of this very influential individual. Of everything I learned about Cyrus Eaton though, there has remained one thought that has permeated the approach I have always taken in business, and although I have never enjoyed the successes achieved by Mr. Eaton, my lack of financial gain has never diminished the value of that one thought.

Primarily, Cyrus Eaton believed that if there was a job to be done somewhere, it was his responsibility as a chief executive, to hire the most competent and able individual capable of fulfilling the responsibilities of that job, pay that individual more money than any competitor would ever imagine paying that person, and then turn that person loose to do the job they were hired to do, without interference.

Cyrus Eaton knew that he did not know how to do everything; he knew that he did not have all the answers. His solution, therefore, was to hire the best available assistants that money could buy, and then set those people free to do the job they were hired to do.

"We the People" need to comprehend the fullness of what Cyrus Eaton instinctively knew, and stop thinking that our President and Vice-President must have all the answers to all the questions. Ms. Palin did not have all the answers, but clearly, by and through her accomplishments, Ms. Palin proved that she knew how to surround herself with the right people. And those people knew how to do their jobs. The results of Ms. Palin's leadership efforts remain unparalleled by any current Governor, Senator or other candidate for the Presidency, including the inept individual currently sitting in that office today! We are in political and financial turmoil today, because we continue hiring demigods, who believe they have all the answers, and who believe they are incapable of failure.

We also arrived at this point, because we naively assume that everybody labors from a base established with honor. Our media laughingly jokes about the lack of honesty and integrity within our political ranks, while "We the People" somehow believe that our elected officials are going to labor in truth, honesty and sincerity as our Constitutional Representatives. And, we keep electing officials with proven "questionable" character traits. Are we really that naïve and irresponsible? Historically, I guess we are!

Throughout history, it could be said that a sense of integrity, and a basic knowledge of right and wrong, was present within the fiber of humanity. The fact of the matter though, is that integrity, honesty, and even the knowledge of right and wrong, started falling apart in the mid 1920's, while the full impact of our shift in morality did not become significantly evident until the mid-1960's. We can also add that the rollercoaster of politics and social grace and integrity literally "topped the hill" during the war in Vietnam.

From that point in time, the silent majority has been driven inward, as they were bombarded with the idiocy taking place around them. In moving inward, the door was left open for a very vocal minority to push along their agendas without too much interference. If you think that is too harsh or wrong, I suggest you spend some serious time evaluating the downward slide of the world since 1965, because things are done today that would never have been considered or tolerated before that time. In spite of that fact, we remain silent!

Simple things, like getting into fights, happened back in the 1950's and 1960's, but back then there was a knowing when to stop. Today, however, fights usually end when someone is either dead, or so severely maimed, that the "loser" in a fight is never the same (mentally or physically). It's not just good enough to defeat a foe; today we are compelled to literally destroy that foe. A perfect example of this occurred last year, when a "fan" was maimed for life, simply because he went to a stadium wearing his "visiting" teams' jersey.

Truly, idiocy rules at many levels, because we allow it! The punishment no longer fits the crime, and matters are worsening in a vast number of areas every day. This is so, because the silent majority has allowed it.

Wow, that's pretty harsh, isn't it? Yes, it is harsh, but it is also true.

Would you like some examples of what I consider to be idiotic? Seriously, are you interested in engaging in a very harsh and controversial social and political conversation? OK, let's get serious:

The silent majority is responsible for the fact that rapists, murderers and others guilty of heinous crimes against society, not only remain alive once proven to be guilty, but many offenders are also allowed to walk the streets of our world without any concern of serious consequences; they are free to repeat their crimes. Think about that for a few minutes, will you?

The bullies are winning as they continually rewrite the laws of our society, and the silent majority has allowed this to happen.

In the last chapter I touched on rape, incest, pedophilia, abduction, and abuse. Well, how about murder? In the past, murder was an offense punishable by death. Nonetheless, murderers today also receive a slap on the wrist for their offense, and are often returned to society within a few years, where they too are free to repeat their crime. Like rapists, or any other heinous offender of society, they all receive, free of charge mind you, everything they might want or need while imprisoned.

Please grasp this fact: Those imprisoned within our country, who have committed horrible and heinous crimes against our citizens, whose crimes should warrant immediate execution, receive instead, an all-inclusive free healthcare package, along with free rent, food, TV entertainment, exercise areas, libraries and computers, to name just a few of their "Benefits". And these perks cost the taxpayers of our country approximately $50,000.00 per year – per prisoner. While this is taking place, we have a massive group of elderly in this nation, who have paid their dues, but who now are forced to live at, or below, poverty levels, without ample insurance or care. Rapists, pedophiles, murderers and whatever other group of social misfits we might choose to name, live without any need whatsoever, at our expense, while our law-abiding seniors live in poverty. And "We the People" allow this nonsense to continue!

How idiotic and passive is that?

Let me add two other examples of this particular idiocy, and I will move on to other topics:

✓ Illegal immigrants <u>imprisoned</u> within the United States receive greater benefits, than disabled American citizens receiving Social Security Disability Insurance (insurance for which those disabled citizens have paid).

✓ Illegal immigrants <u>on welfare</u> within the United States of America receive greater benefits, than disabled American citizens receiving Social Security Disability Insurance (insurance, again, for which those disabled citizens have paid).

There is something outrageously wrong with all of these scenario's, but until the silent majority decides to do something about these matters, "We the People" of the United States will continue to live in a world driven by this kind of absurd leadership.

Self-interest, greed, oppressive power, unjust socialistic judicial rulings, and any other number of self-serving matters are ruining our nation and world, and just like the events leading to the Holocaust of World War II, the silent majority is allowing these things to happen today! The result of our continued silence is going to allow a repeat of that Holocaust horror in much greater proportions.

Let me repeat that: Unless the silent majority, and all correct thinking individuals within our nation and world, becomes willing to engage and remain silent no more, there will be a repeat of the Holocaust of World War II, in greater proportions. The question you need to ask yourself is, "Who will be the target of the next holocaust?" You? Maybe. Me? Probably so, especially if I continue speaking forth in this manner!

Once "Martial Law" is proclaimed by this president, should he somehow be reelected, Homeland Security will be turned loose upon all who are willing to take a stand against Socialism and Totalitarianism, and the next political Holocaust will be underway!

Personally, I am willing to engage today, at whatever level is needed, in defense of the Constitution I swore to defend and uphold, while also pursuing and upholding the self-worth and value of every person. The fact is, however, a very select group, a very vocal minority, is ruling and dominating our nation and our world. Unless the silent majority becomes willing to engage in upholding and defending the Constitution, along with those already engaged in this fight, then the United States, as we know it, will no longer exist.

It is also true, and frightening as well, that when the United States ultimately falls, which it will without our active involvement, Democracy, as we know it, along with the freedom and liberties which that democracy provide, and to which we have grown accustomed, will fall worldwide.

The failure we are witnessing within society is the fact that too many of the naturally "passive" personalities on the conservative and rational side of practically every issue, have either forgotten how to positively engage in the proper maintenance of those issues, have acquired so much complacent comfort – as to sincerely believe the approaching doom cannot touch them – or have simply surrendered their viewpoint to their opponents, and are "passively" living with the results.

Bluntly put, that is an appalling thing!

"We the People" need to be willing to make a fist and take a stand against the idiocy currently ruling our society and destroying our nation, today! Surprisingly, the truth of it all is that it really will not take much to make the changes. One punch is all that was needed for Bradley to be free from his tormentor. One punch! Was he punished for taking his stand? You bet he was. But in the long run, life has been much better for Bradley.

The same truth is going to apply to us as well, because we must pay a price for allowing idiocy to reign so long. Getting "out of the red", because we are in fact a very deeply indebted nation, is going to take some serious work. (We are NOT bankrupt though, in spite of what you are hearing). But unless we are willing to elect officials who will seriously work toward the goals **WE** establish, which in this particular instance MUST include a balanced budget amendment, and unless we are willing to impeach (kick out of office) those officials who refuse to fulfill our wishes, then we are going to continue down this same path, and a once free nation, and the light of the world, is going to be extinguished.

Furthermore, our impeachment process must include judges at every level, including the Supreme Court, when those judges change the laws of the land, in order to force the will of the majority to conform to their view of society. The Constitution of the United States is not negotiable. "We the People" are in charge. "We the People" decide. "We the People" dictate and determine.

Why have we surrendered those rights, and will we ever be willing to engage again to regain and defend those very rights?

I am amused to see the very liberal elite seeking to impeach members of the Supreme Court, because that court deferred the Obama healthcare program back to the States. The members of the court rightly determined that Obamacare was a State by State matter, and in so correctly determining, the "left" is throwing a temper tantrum!

My sincerest hope is that the thoughts I am expressing will awaken the rage that should exist within each one of us, and impel, compel, and propel each of us to become willing to engage on behalf of that which is morally right; on behalf of that which is, at its base, laden with the integrity now lacking throughout our political leadership groups.

Politics 101, in my thinking, is about "We the People", because until "We the People" reclaim our nation and heritage, "We the People" will remain stuck in the morass that currently rules, and doom is at the end of our current path.

Want another issue to discuss? OK, let's talk about our economy:

➤ Do you know that one of the largest single oilfields ever discovered in the world, sits under North Dakota, South Dakota, Montana and Wyoming? This particular "find" has a couple of names, but it is commonly referred to as the Bakken Shale Play. And further, do you know that another new massive oilfield has also been found under the Rocky Mountains? Due to technological advances, these "Shale Oil" discoveries make these "finds" very easy to tap. Furthermore, those same technological advances are promoting a complete resurgence of crude oil processing throughout Texas, Oklahoma, Louisiana, California, Pennsylvania and Ohio.

Of equal importance is the fact that natural gas discoveries under all these new and old oilfields, plus our proven coal reserves, signify that the United States remains very rich in natural resources. The United States IS an oil independent nation provided we are allowed to refine and process our own natural resources.

So what is stopping "We the People" from working our way out from under the heavy hand of OPEC; out from under a bludgeoning trade deficit, and out from under an ever expanding and oppressive National Debt?

Congresswoman, Maxine Waters (D), California, in a very recent Congressional Hearing, openly stated, in regard to the drilling requests being made by the oil companies (to tap into our proven reserves), that the "Liberal Agenda" is to "Socialize" our oil industry. In response to a guarantee of lower gas prices, made by John Hofmeister, President of Shell Oil Company, congresswoman Waters said, **"This Liberal would be about Socializi--. Basically, this Liberal would be about taking over, and the government running all of your companies."***

Do you understand the implications of that statement? If the citizens of California, who are represented by this "Liberal Socialist", do not impeach this woman immediately, then those citizens are telling the rest of the nation that they are in agreement with that socialistic agenda, and we must beware! Our Constitution is being threatened today by enemies both "Foreign and Domestic", in ways never before seen. Personally, I am deeply concerned.

[Conversations and debate rage occasionally about a State or States wanting to secede from the Union; wanting to disengage as a member of the United States, and become an independent nation. The Supreme Court waffles on the constitutionality of such matters, but according to the Constitution, States may in fact secede from the Union, if they so choose.

Furthermore, the president of the United States today is seeking to have Arizona removed from the rolls of the Union in a reverse secession, because Arizona has taken a no-nonsense approach to illegal immigration. The president does not like being defied in this way, so he is seeking a backdoor "punishment" for all six million Arizonan's, as he seeks to disengage Arizona from the United States.

My question though, is a bit different: "What do 'We the People' need to do to force the removal of a State or States – from the rolls of the Union, and kick that State or States OUT?"

It is increasingly clear that California, for instance, politically stands in opposition to the majority of this great nation. Yet the power wielded by that state plays a significant role in the political direction we are forced to take. So, once the silent majority has had enough of California's antics, what would it take for us to tell them to either shape-up, or "Go Away!"???]

On top of an extremely anti-American and anti-Constitutional Liberal agenda, we have a massive group of "Environmentalists", who are also fighting against the drilling of our proven reserves. Would you like to know why the environmentalists are fighting against our pumping that oil? In a word: Money! The OPEC nations are feeding multiple hundreds of millions of dollars into those environmental agencies (Lobbyists) every year, enabling those people to lobby here in the United States, against our drilling our own oil reserves. Why? Because once we tap into our resources, we can tell OPEC to shove their $110.00 per barrel oil up their own resource!

The oilfields of the Dakotas, the Rockies, Alaska, Texas, Oklahoma, California, Pennsylvania, Louisiana, Ohio, and others as well, including our already discovered offshore reserves, can fuel the needs of our nation for centuries. Did you get that? As a nation, if we manage our resources properly, we can be oil independent for hundreds of years. So why aren't we independent? Why aren't we pumping our reserves? Why aren't we creating homegrown jobs? Why aren't we getting out of debt, instead of increasing our massive debts on a daily basis?

Primarily, we are not using every possible tool available to us today, to cure most of our social and economic ills, because an agenda exists to alter the very fiber of our society, and a very

140

insidious minority of very vocal extremists, are currently pulling our strings. We are being conditioned to believe many absurd things today, and as the silent majority idly and quietly sits, our Democratic Republic is slowly being turned into a Socialistic Totalitarian State...

Considering the fact that the "at the pump" price for Regular gasoline, transported from the Middle East, was only $1.50 per gallon a couple of years ago, and considering the fact that the global economy has been stagnant, and inflation has not existed for years, then we must conclude that the oil companies CAN be very profitable at that $1.50 per gallon price. Perfect! Then let's begin at that point, and allow our domestic producers to enjoy whatever profit they can squeeze from that $1.50 per gallon price.

But, we cannot stop there.

Because of our indebtedness, "We the People" can dictate that we want our resources managed properly and wisely, using common sense. And, in the use of our resources, we want to add a $2.50 per gallon tax at the pump, stipulating that 90% of those tax dollars be used ONLY to pay down our National debt, while the other 10% is to be used for that same debt pay-down within the State in which the gasoline is purchased. And yes, that means that we will be paying a firm, "at the pump" price of $4.00 per gallon (Regular and Diesel) for the sweet crude that <u>we own.</u> Once the debts are eliminated, however, the tax is also eliminated.

Sadly though, we owe a lot of money! Our national debt is currently approaching $15 trillion dollars!

According to the US Energy Information Administration, the United States consumes 137.76 billion gallons of gasoline each year. At $2.50 per gallon in taxation, we would be paying approximately $345 billion dollars per year against our National and State debts. IF we implemented and maintained balanced budgets throughout the Nation and States, and if we did not contribute to the pay down of our debt from any other sources, this tax would eliminate our National and State debts in approximately FIFTY YEARS!

That is how deeply in debt we are! The above sort of program, however, must stipulate that all interest due on the current debt be paid within the balanced budgets of the States and the Nation. The tax pays down the debt. PERIOD!

While fifty years is better than never, it remains an unacceptable timeframe for getting out of debt. We can do better! Fortunately for us, there are other positive economical solutions available to us as well, and there are people within this nation who have greater knowledge of these matters than me. But, are we listening? Are we sincerely attempting to engage alongside of these reasonable and responsible constitutionally minded citizens, in order to eliminate the oppressive and suppressive agenda that is currently being leveled against us?

In further thought, as we pay down our debt, we can use the money we save on interest payments currently paid against that debt, and finance research and development of alternative energy sources, so that within twenty-five years, we won't have to use our petroleum reserves to the extent we do today. We can begin saving that resource for production of items requiring petroleum only – for countless future generations.

By acting rationally, we can motivate research, create jobs, and preserve our petroleum reserves for many future generations. And the more we advance in our technologies, the less dependence we will have on that petroleum resource.

The means are available today though, to tell OPEC, and every other source of oil, that they either reduce the price of their crude oil significantly, back to the point that allowed for the $1.50 per gallon level, or we begin pumping! The only question is: Are "We the People" willing to engage in a battle against the lobbyists and corrupt anti-American, anti-Constitution politicians, and take back our country? Are we willing to sacrifice oil flow from OPEC, until we generate full flow of our own oil sources, and reclaim that which our own citizens are trying to subvert?

➢ In line with technological advances though, I think it is time for "We the People" to ask why things are backing up at the

U.S. Patent office. Why is it that so many patent applications for technological advances, which would generate jobs and reduce our dependency on petroleum usage, are not receiving their patents? Who is pulling the strings and stopping "We the People" from moving forward?

Here is more food for thought:

➢ Perhaps the single most ignorant political act in the last fifty years was the manner in which "Washington" indebted us in an absolutely futile bank "bailout program". An even larger act of political arrogance is looming with the proposed medical insurance program.

Building bridges and repairing roads, as part of the bailout, are wonderful things, but every time I see a sign along the road that boasts about how we are "Putting America Back to Work", I want to throw-up. Aside from the fact that construction of that nature is temporary; construction is a Band-Aid, please do not lose sight of the fact that our Government (State and Federal) is using foreign companies, who are importing foreign labor, to complete many of those infrastructure repairs... How stupid is that?

Nevertheless, once a bridge is repaired, it remains in wonderful condition for decades. Although road and bridge repair is essential, because our infrastructure IS falling apart, those are not the type of jobs we need today. We need manufacturing jobs that fuel local and federal economies. We need manufacturing jobs that permanently employ multiple-millions of Americans, and which allow those working Americans to purchase food and clothing for their families, as well as to purchase homes, cars, boats, RV's, and other things that keep other people working. We need manufacturing jobs that allow for greater exports. We do not need Band-Aids.

Do you know that *__for the most part__*, we do not manufacture shoes or clothing in the United States of America today? It's true! The same is true for dozens of other industries. While we may produce minimum amounts of shoes and clothing within our borders, it is clear that these, and vast numbers of many different types of manufacturing facilities, have moved offshore. We need to bring those manufacturing plants, and jobs, back to the United States. We need to promote programs that will provide permanent manufacturing jobs for our citizens.

Do you want an effective program from our Government? Then insist we move away from the bailout mentality completely, and initiate "Stimulus Programs", that will actually accomplish something.

In this vein, as an example, how about lending money, interest free for ten or fifteen years, to manufacturing companies, thereby providing a wonderful incentive for manufacturers to build new plants, with new equipment, here in the United States. Applying a maximum 25% corporate tax upon the profits earned by all corporations within our country, and eliminating oppressive and restrictive regulatory taxes and laws currently in place, we will actually allow our manufacturers, and their investor shareholders, to earn an income. This stimulus program would create permanent jobs, paying permanent salaries and permanent taxes to Local, State and Federal coffers. The original money loaned is repaid, jobs are created, our growth and trade imbalances are favorably impacted, and our National and State debts are ultimately eliminated.

Furthermore, within the contracts for this sort of stimulus program, we stipulate that all equipment needed within those new manufacturing facilities (whenever possible) must be "Made in America", and in so doing we stimulate our heavy equipment manufacturing sector at the same time. Should we so choose, we can also offer additional incentives to manufacturers who are willing to renovate abandoned factories within the country, and thereby revitalize neighborhoods, and remove the blithe from our land.

It must be noted at this point, however, that many of the things I am suggesting are not new. The most remarkable aspect to all of this though, is the fact that "Conservative Republicans" have been advocating these types of changes for decades, but the Blue Collar Workers of America primarily vote for the "Liberal Democrats", who are slowly selling-off everything those Blue Collar Workers hold near and dear. Yes folks, it really is the "Liberal Democrats" who are primarily responsible for the deplorable condition of our workforce today! And, the current administration is "selling-out" America faster than any other administration in history...

[As I have said, I was born and raised in Cleveland, Ohio. I still consider Cleveland my earth-born home. But, I must confess that I am greatly disappointed by the people of Cleveland (and Detroit, and any number of other large ex-industrial hubs), who continually vote for Democratic leadership at the local and city levels, and expect a change in the deplorable conditions of those cities. Nothing is going to change, until YOU change your minds about who you are and what you want to accomplish in your lives. If you continue doing the same things, the same things will continue happening. And liberalism with regard to our economies and welfare is killing our cities and nation.]

With that said, and with all that has been offered herein, it is not impossible to envision how resolving the fuel issue (Use, Price, Tax), combined with the proper repair of our manufacturing issues, can actually put this nation back to work and out of debt within a relatively reasonable period of time! And, once we are debt free, or close to being debt free, including the aforementioned repayment of all Social Security and Medicare funds, we can take a serious look at how we manage healthcare and medical insurance as a whole. We can sensibly secure ample healthcare benefits for every citizen of this great nation, without indebting countless future generations in the process.

It all sounds too easy doesn't it? Well, in truth, it could be that easy! "We the People" can make it that easy.

If we build for the future, and not for the instant, we can sustain long term gains worldwide. But in order to accomplish the task, we must stop thinking that everything is free; we must stop thinking that we are 'entitled' to things that we have not earned. The proposed medical insurance program currently under debate fits right in with the entitlement thinking that is rampant today, and it must be shut down now, before our entire medical community ends in ruin, and our States and Nation end in total economic chaos.

The proposed medical insurance program will bankrupt every State, as well as bankrupt the Nation. The program itself, and the manner in which it was enforced, is a perfect example of an administration that is quickly turning into a dictatorship, and follows a pattern that is fully anti-American, anti-Christian, anti-everything reasonable, responsible, patriotic or righteous, as well as anti-Constitutional. In spite of these truths, this administration, and its medical insurance program, is still supported by a very vocal minority of the voluntarily blind, who in turn are leading the masses of those people who insatiably desire increased entitlements. And the populace simply will not open their eyes to the realities of life today. "We the People" cannot tolerate a greater indebtedness at any level: State or National. But unless we engage in the battle raging about us, we will not survive as a free land.

There are no "fixes" available that are not going to require an all-out effort. There are no "entitlements" without a cost. Nothing will ever change though, unless "We the People" become "Willing To Engage and remain Silent No More!

*The fact that an agenda is already in place to "Socialize" American industry, by a very Liberal political and social group of individuals, is not a secret. I am stunned, however, by the fact that "We the People" are surrendering our freedoms and liberties without a fight. While I have tried to NOT discuss the current presidential administration (and I refuse to "capitalize" those words in reference to "this group"), the open statement of "Socializing" our industries by Maxine Waters, should not only enrage every citizen of the United States, but should cause the world to tremble.

Listed in Glossary I are some very important definitions that "We the People" must truly and fully understand. The first three words form a base from which we must begin, because they define who and what we are (supposed to be) as a nation today. The final three words outline the direction which that very select Liberal group is trying to drive this Democratic Republic.

In understanding these six words, I am asking the people of America to decide which form of Government they want for our future, because the outcome of every election, as well as the judicial and civic appointments made by those we elect, have and will determine the very nature of our country. <u>This is especially true for the elections taking place in November of 2012</u>. And if you think your vote does not count, then you have just reduced yourself to zero. Your coin, in this regard, is useless!

If you are not seeing or hearing what I am trying to say, let me phrase this differently: I, and many others, am openly stating that the current presidential administration, along with the majority of those currently holding office within the House of Representatives and The U.S. Senate, along with certain members of the Supreme Court, are intentionally usurping the Constitution of the United States. By their own words and deeds they daily provide proof, that they are indeed, Socialistic Totalitarians. And their intent, should the current president somehow get reelected, is to end the Democratic Republic of the United States of America!

I can make it no clearer than that…

Please permit me to end this chapter with this note on our voting processes, because these thoughts surely do belong under the heading, "Politics 101":

There is a very large group of citizens who believe that our "Electronic voting systems" open the door for fraud and the mishandling of our ballots. Further, as evidenced by the "Chad" incident in Florida a few years ago, even that system is under suspicion. Additionally, many citizens have tremendous doubt over the validity and integrity of the voting taking place within California, for instance, because it is believed that the State of California is actively permitting, and promoting, voting by illegal immigrants. Whether these suspicions are true or not, is irrelevant. What is relevant though, is that in order to promote active participation by every citizen, including the silent majority, we must eliminate all suspicions surrounding our voting processes.

To this end I offer the following solutions:

First: Return all ballots to the "old" pencil in the circle (Mark the spot) ballot form. Electronic voting is fast and efficient, but electronic voting is also subject to manipulation, and therefore, will always generate results that are "suspect" in nature. We must remove that suspicion completely.

Second: Position National Guard or Regular Military personnel at each polling place, and have these armed guards oversee, protect, and insure the integrity of each ballot box. This ballot protection must include accompanying the ballot boxes to wherever the votes are physically counted, once the polls do close and the balloting is complete. 24/7 military protection of all ballot boxes, ballots, and the counting process, insures the integrity of our votes, once the votes are cast.

➢ While there are a number of questionable situations taking place today, as recently as 1946, in what is known as "The Battle of Athens, TN", the use of military force was needed to insure the validity of our ballot processes. The link provided here offers a very powerful statement regarding this matter: http://voxvocispublicus.homestead.com/Battle-of-Athens.html

Third: Film the entire voting process at every facility, including the transport and final counting process of every ballot box. Filming our entire process further insures the integrity of the vote, and the technology exists to provide for this safeguard, without tremendous expense.

Fourth: Demand proof of citizenship from every voter (Birth Certificate and a Government issued photo ID; Driver's license, State ID, or Passport ID). Proof of citizenship is mandated by our Constitution, and we must uphold that mandate.

Fifth, insist that until the polls close on the West Coast, that absolutely NO final count results of ANY local, city or state be released. "We the People" cannot be concerned with how the media chooses to cover and project the results of OUR elections. But, by allowing East Coast results to be broadcast before all polling places close on the West Coast, we unduly influence the vote still taking place in those different time zones.

148

A great deal is at stake in every election; the very form of our government hangs in the balance of our vote. The processes used to gather and count our vote, therefore, must be beyond reproach. "We the People" must demand the fullness of these matters, because "We the People" ARE the government, and our voice must be heard!]

(Thomas Jefferson)

"To compel a man to furnish funds for the propagation of ideas he disbelieves and abhors is sinful and tyrannical."

(C. S. Lewis)

"What I want to fix your attention on is the vast overall movement towards the discrediting, and finally the elimination, of every kind of human excellence − moral, cultural, social or intellectual. And is it not pretty to notice how 'democracy' (in the incantatory sense) is now doing for us the work that was once done by the most ancient dictatorships, and by the same methods? The basic proposal of the new education is to be that dunces and idlers must not be made to feel inferior to intelligent, and idlers must not be made to feel inferior to intelligent and industrious pupils. That would be 'undemocratic'. Children who are fit to proceed may be artificially kept back, because the others would get a trauma by being left behind. The bright pupil thus remains democratically fettered to his own age group throughout his school career, and a boy who would be capable of tackling Aeschylus or Dante sits listening to his coeval's attempts to spell out A CAT SAT ON A MAT. We may reasonably hope for the virtual abolition of education when 'I'm as good as you' has fully had its way. All incentives to learn and all penalties for not learning will vanish. The few who might want to learn will be prevented; who are they to overtop their fellows? And anyway, the teachers − or should I say nurses? − will be far too busy reassuring the dunces and patting them on the back to waste any time on real teaching. We shall no longer have to plan and toil to spread imperturbable conceit and incurable ignorance among men."

Epilogue:
The Declaration of Independence
and
The 7th Column Movement™

C ontained within this Epilogue is the Declaration of Independence of the United States of America. This declaration was adopted by Congress on July 4, 1776, and it announced to the world, the reason for the separation of the thirteen colonies from Great Britain, and the establishment of the United States of America. I sincerely hope you will read this document in its entirety.

The last sentence of the Declaration reads, "And for the support of this declaration, with a firm reliance on the protection of Divine Providence, we mutually pledge to each other our lives, our fortunes and our sacred honor." And, following the Declaration are the names of the original 56 signee's of the document. Of those 56 men, five were captured by the British as traitors, and tortured before they died. Twelve had their homes destroyed. Two lost their sons serving in the Revolutionary Army, while another had two sons captured. Nine of the 56 fought and died from wounds or hardships of the Revolutionary War. Most ultimately died in poverty, having lost all of their personal wealth, belongings and, in many instances, their families as well.

So, the question I have for you today as we discuss the realities of being "Willing To Engage"; in the knowledge of the Patriot Act, the gradual erosion of liberties that we have already experienced, as well as the constant threat to our First and Second Amendment rights, plus the threatened socialization of our medical and industrial institutions, is:

"In light of the ultimate fate of the original 56 signers of the Declaration of Independence, <u>how willing are you to sign this document right now</u>, realizing that there might be additional responsibilities required for the continued defense and affirmation of our inalienable rights?"

More conversation follows the Declaration of Independence, so please read on:

Declaration of Independence

Here is the complete text of the Declaration of Independence. (The original spelling and capitalization have been retained.)

(Adopted by Congress on July 4, 1776)

The Unanimous Declaration
of the Thirteen United States of America

When, in the course of human events, it becomes necessary for one people to dissolve the political bands which have connected them with another, and to assume among the powers of the earth, the separate and equal station to which the laws of nature and of nature's God entitle them, a decent respect to the opinions of mankind requires that they should declare the causes which impel them to the separation.

We hold these truths to be self-evident, that all men are created equal, that they are endowed by their Creator with certain unalienable rights, that among these are life, liberty and the pursuit of happiness. That to secure these rights, governments are instituted among men, deriving their just powers from the consent of the governed. That whenever any form of government becomes destructive to these ends, it is the right of the people to alter or to abolish it, and to institute new government, laying its foundation on such principles and organizing its powers in such form, as to them shall seem most likely to effect their safety and happiness. Prudence, indeed, will dictate that governments long established should not be changed for light and transient causes; and accordingly all experience hath shown that mankind are more disposed to suffer, while evils are sufferable, than to right themselves by abolishing the forms to which they are accustomed. But when a long train of abuses and usurpations, pursuing invariably the same object evinces a design to reduce them under absolute despotism, it is their right, it is their duty, to throw off such government, and to provide new guards for their future security. -- Such has been the patient sufferance of these colonies; and such is now the necessity which constrains them to alter their former systems of government. The history of the present King of Great Britain is a history of repeated injuries and usurpations, all having in direct object the establishment of an absolute tyranny over these states. To prove this, let facts be submitted to a candid world.

He has refused his assent to laws, the most wholesome and necessary for the public good.

He has forbidden his governors to pass laws of immediate and pressing importance, unless suspended in their operation till his assent should be obtained; and when so suspended, he has utterly neglected to attend to them.

He has refused to pass other laws for the accommodation of large districts of people, unless those people would relinquish the right of representation in the legislature, a right inestimable to them and formidable to tyrants only.

He has called together legislative bodies at places unusual, uncomfortable, and distant from the depository of their public records, for the sole purpose of fatiguing them into compliance with his measures.

He has dissolved representative houses repeatedly, for opposing with manly firmness his invasions on the rights of the people.

He has refused for a long time, after such dissolutions, to cause others to be elected; whereby the legislative powers, incapable of annihilation, have returned to the people at large for their exercise; the state remaining in the meantime exposed to all the dangers of invasion from without, and convulsions within.

He has endeavored to prevent the population of these states; for that purpose obstructing the laws for naturalization of foreigners; refusing to pass others to encourage their migration hither, and raising the conditions of new appropriations of lands.

He has obstructed the administration of justice, by refusing his assent to laws for establishing judiciary powers.

He has made judges dependent on his will alone, for the tenure of their offices, and the amount and payment of their salaries.

He has erected a multitude of new offices, and sent hither swarms of officers to harass our people, and eat out their substance.

He has kept among us, in times of peace, standing armies without the consent of our legislature.

He has affected to render the military independent of and superior to civil power.

He has combined with others to subject us to a jurisdiction foreign to our constitution, and unacknowledged by our laws; giving his assent to their acts of pretended legislation:

For quartering large bodies of armed troops among us:

For protecting them, by mock trial, from punishment for any murders which they should commit on the inhabitants of these states:

For cutting off our trade with all parts of the world:

For imposing taxes on us without our consent:

For depriving us in many cases, of the benefits of trial by jury:

For transporting us beyond seas to be tried for pretended offenses:

For abolishing the free system of English laws in a neighboring province, establishing therein an arbitrary government, and enlarging its boundaries so as to render it at once an example and fit instrument for introducing the same absolute rule in these colonies:

For taking away our charters, abolishing our most valuable laws, and altering fundamentally the forms of our governments:

For suspending our own legislatures, and declaring themselves invested with power to legislate for us in all cases whatsoever.

He has abdicated government here, by declaring us out of his protection and waging war against us.

He has plundered our seas, ravaged our coasts, burned our towns, and destroyed the lives of our people.

He is at this time transporting large armies of foreign mercenaries to complete the works of death, desolation and tyranny, already begun with circumstances of cruelty and perfidy scarcely paralleled in the most barbarous ages, and totally unworthy the head of a civilized nation.

He has constrained our fellow citizens taken captive on the high seas to bear arms against their country, to become the executioners of their friends and brethren, or to fall themselves by their hands.

He has excited domestic insurrections amongst us, and has endeavored to bring on the inhabitants of our frontiers, the merciless Indian savages, whose known rule of warfare, is undistinguished destruction of all ages, sexes and conditions.

In every stage of these oppressions we have petitioned for redress in the most humble terms: our repeated petitions have been answered only by repeated injury. A prince, whose character is thus marked by every act which may define a tyrant, is unfit to be the ruler of a free people.

Nor have we been wanting in attention to our British brethren. We have warned them from time to time of attempts by their legislature to extend an unwarrantable jurisdiction over us. We have reminded them of the circumstances of our emigration and settlement here. We have appealed to their native justice and magnanimity, and we have conjured them by the ties of our common kindred to disavow these usurpations, which, would inevitably interrupt our connections and correspondence. They too have been deaf to the voice of justice and of consanguinity. We must, therefore, acquiesce in the necessity, which denounces our separation, and hold them, as we hold the rest of mankind, enemies in war, in peace friends.

We, therefore, the representatives of the United States of America, in General Congress, assembled, appealing to the Supreme Judge of the world for the rectitude of our intentions, do, in the name, and by the authority of the good people of these colonies, solemnly publish and declare, that these united colonies are, and of right ought to be free and independent states; that they are absolved from all allegiance to the British Crown, and that all political connection between them and the state of Great Britain, is and ought to be totally dissolved; and that as free and independent states, they have full power to levy war, conclude peace, contract alliances, establish commerce, and to do all other acts and things which independent states may of right do. And for the support of this declaration, with a firm reliance on the protection of Divine Providence, we mutually pledge to each other our lives, our fortunes and our sacred honor.

Source: The Pennsylvania Packet, July 8, 1776

The 56 signatures on the Declaration appear in the positions indicated:

Column 1
Georgia:
Button Gwinnett
Lyman Hall
George Walton

Column 2
North Carolina:
William Hooper
Joseph Hewes
John Penn
South Carolina:
Edward Rutledge
Thomas Heyward, Jr.
Thomas Lynch, Jr.
Arthur Middleton

Column 3
Massachusetts:
John Hancock
Maryland:
Samuel Chase
William Paca
Thomas Stone
Charles Carroll of Carrollton
Virginia:
George Wythe
Richard Henry Lee
Thomas Jefferson
Benjamin Harrison
Thomas Nelson, Jr.
Francis Lightfoot Lee
Carter Braxton

Column 4
Pennsylvania:
Robert Morris
Benjamin Rush
Benjamin Franklin
John Morton
George Clymer
James Smith
George Taylor
James Wilson
George Ross
Delaware:
Caesar Rodney
George Read
Thomas McKean

Column 5
New York:
William Floyd
Philip Livingston
Francis Lewis
Lewis Morris
New Jersey:
Richard Stockton

John Witherspoon
Francis Hopkinson
John Hart
Abraham Clark

Column 6
New Hampshire:
Josiah Bartlett
William Whipple
Massachusetts:
Samuel Adams
John Adams
Robert Treat Paine
Elbridge Gerry
Rhode Island:
Stephen Hopkins
William Ellery
Connecticut:
Roger Sherman
Samuel Huntington
William Williams
Oliver Wolcott
New Hampshire:
Matthew Thornton

As I sat looking at The Declaration, and as I looked upon the names and the literal six columns containing their signatures, I could not help but wonder: Do we dare consider adding an unofficial Column 7 to this document today, in our hearts and in our minds, in order to commit ourselves to the preservation and restoration of our Constitution, and this Declaration of Independence? Do we dare NOT engage in an effort to uphold and defend all that makes the United States of America the land of the free, and the home of the brave? And if we choose to remain silent and surrender the liberties and freedoms, for which so many have offered the ultimate sacrifice of their lives, how do we (how can we) look our children and grandchildren in the eye and explain our unwillingness to engage on their behalf?

The very value and self-worth of each individual is indelibly written within the pages of the documents I have quoted throughout this writing. And it is the fullness of that value and self-worth that is being threatened today by the bullies and extremists who wish to alter our history, diminish the intent of those documents, and forever eliminate that which this book (and others, to be sure) is striving to maintain.

In the ninth grade I knew I had value and self-worth, and no one was going to take those basic beliefs from me; not then, and certainly not now. The question you must ask yourself right now, though, is;

"How willing am I to engage in the defense of my own value and self-worth, as well as the value and self-worth of my children, my grandchildren and countless generations to come? How "Willing To Engage", and remain "Silent No More", am I going to be, as we legitimately and actively fight for the return of sanity and common sense in our government, our society, and our world?"

I had no idea that this is where my prequel to "A Diamond on The Wall" was heading. I had no preconceived plan to introduce anything of this sort when I began talking about my childhood, or when I dredged up the unpleasant memories of my tumultuous years, and actually exposed those matters to you. I had no notion that this book was going to transition from my childhood, through my harsh teen years, and into a call to arms for civil action in such a forceful way.

The notion of a 7th Column of Signatures is beyond me. The fact that there are others more qualified to speak on political issues; on social issues; on economic issues, is extremely obvious as well. Unquestionably, there are others today who are more involved in correcting many of the ills of our society and governments.

But here I am, extremely tired of being bullied by an incompetent, self-centered, narcissistic, self-serving and inept vocal minority, who are trying to destroy everything and everyone that I believe have incalculable value and worth (which would be YOU, our nation, and the world community). I simply cannot remain static, quiet or uninvolved. It is not in my nature to remain unattached. Like you, I have been pushed to the floor, but I am not going to be docile. I must be true to who I am, and what I have become, and in the totality of it all, I am willing to engage with every ounce of strength, to seek our victory over those bullies.

If you are willing, please join with me, and allow your "voice" to be added as a statement to our leaders (worldwide), that we shall remain silent no more. There is nothing physical to sign. There is no concern for retribution. What I have conceived is a very simple means whereby, "We the People" can tell our leaders that we are once again willing to engage on behalf of that which is right, fair, just and true.

By visiting the website I recently established: www.7thcolumnmovement.com you will activate the counter at the site, and through that count, as each person visits, will be "signing" a rhetorical 7th Column of names to The Declaration of Independence. Additionally, by visiting the site, you are making a conscious vow to yourself, that you are willing to engage in the defense of your own self-worth and value. You are making a conscious vow to get involved, even if that involvement extends only to the point of knowledgeably voting.

I promise that by visiting this site, there will be no cookies, attachments, pop-ups, or anything that can be harmful or injurious to you, or to your computer system. I will provide links to other pages for volunteering, for political action groups, and for useful information. I will also provide links for the purchase of this book and my other works as well. Eventually, I will offer links to other valuable works.

By visiting the **7thcolumnmovement.com** website, however, you will make an "electronic" vow and statement against tyranny and oppression, while also stating your intent to maintain and uphold the tenets of freedom and liberty for all.

The Boston Tea Party was a good beginning to the protest movement against "taxation without representation". The

Declaration of Independence, and the Constitution of the United States of America, however, is the culmination of that protest, and the beginning of a wondrous new nation. It is time for our wondrous new nation to be rediscovered in accordance with the intent of our founding fathers, which I have quoted throughout this book!

"We the People" must take control of our nation once again, on behalf of all mankind, because if the beacon of our light is extinguished in our lifetime, then we will have failed our founders, and our God, in whom they placed all hope and trust, and we – above all – shall bear a tremendous blame!

May God truly bless America once again, but may America truly bless our God (in whom we trust) once again as well.

Column 7 - 2012

Lawrence Vosen

The 7th Column Movement™

(Benjamin Franklin)

"At twenty years of age the will reigns; at thirty, the wit; and at forty, the judgment."

(Robert Maynard Hutchins)

"The death of democracy is not likely to be an assassination from ambush. It will be a slow extinction from apathy, indifference, and undernourishment."

(Alexis de Tocqueville)

"Democracy and socialism have nothing in common but one word, equality. But notice the difference: while democracy seeks equality in liberty, socialism seeks equality in restraint and servitude."

(Thomas Sowell)

"Socialism in general has a record of failure so blatant that only an intellectual could ignore or evade it."

ORGANIZATIONS AND WEBSITES:

♥ Abortion – Alternatives:

Adopt Help: http://www.adopthelp.com/?gclid=CKrp-MG_ha8CFWcHRQodMkts4g

Crisis Pregnancy Centers: Over 750 locations within the United States, and over 200 locations in Canada.

♥ Anything / Anywhere:

I visited the AARP.org website http://www.aarp.org/

And from that page I found another link to their, "Giving Back" page: http://www.aarp.org/giving-back/

From that page you can select any number of areas of interest, from Volunteering, to Advocacy, to Community Service, to Charitable Giving and finally, to a page entitled, "Local Heroes", which not only shows how people are trying to change the world (and succeeding), but where assistance is needed in any number of other areas of interest, for those willing to engage!

♥ BULLYING:

The Bully Project: http://www.thebullyproject.com/

♥ Children (Boys and Girls):

Boys and Girls Club of America:
http://www.bgca.org/Pages/index.aspx

Big Brothers and Big Sisters:
http://www.bbbs.org/site/c.9iILI3NGKhK6F/b.5962335/k.BE16/Home.htm

♥ Where Handicapped Can Volunteer:

http://money.howstuffworks.com/economics/volunteer/information/where-handicapped-can-volunteer.htm

♥ **Housing:**

Habitat for Humanity at:
http://www.habitat.org/default.aspx?tgs=NC81LzIwMTIgMTA6MDQ6NTcgQU0%3d

♥ **Hunger and Feeding of the poor, homeless and elderly:**

Feeding America.com:
http://feedingamerica.org/get-involved/volunteer.aspx

Meals on Wheels: http://www.mowaa.org/

♥ **Military:** Assisting organizations who work with our military – and our veterans…

The home page for ourmilitary.mil http://www.ourmilitary.mil/ provides a comprehensive list of community support groups from which you can choose an area of participation if this is where your heart is led to become involved. That list of community support groups can be found at: http://www.ourmilitary.mil/comprehensive-list-of-community-support-groups/

At their National Resource Directory, ourmilitary.mil provides a page that offers all sorts of "Volunteer Opportunities":
https://www.nationalresourcedirectory.gov/volunteer_opportunities

WIKIPEDIA offers a massive list of Veteran Organizations from around the world. This is a link to that page, from which you can investigate any number of Veteran assistance organizations – all seeking volunteers:
http://en.wikipedia.org/wiki/List_of_veterans'_organizations

♥ **News**: And leads to other areas of support:

Fox News: http://www.foxnews.com/

MSNBC has a website that is especially geared toward, "MAKING A DIFFERENCE", which clearly is their way of helping us as we become, "Willing To Engage".
http://www.msnbc.msn.com/id/40153870/ns/nightly_news-making_a_difference/

♥ **Political involvement – at many levels:**
Alan Keyes – Loyal to Liberty
http://loyaltoliberty.com/

Christians and Political Involvement:
http://www.azpolicypages.com/civics-101/christians-and-political-involvement/

Focus on the Family provides information for those seeking to contact their legislative leaders, as well as provides data on how to testify at legislative hearings:
http://www.focusonthefamily.com/socialissues/how-to-make-a-difference.aspx

For Christ and Culture:
http://forchristandculture.com/2011/09/01/no-political-involvement-sin/

Sarah Palin's – Sarahpac:
http://www.sarahpac.com/

Tea Party Patriots: https://www.teapartypatriots.org/

♥ **Pro-Family Organizations and Networks:**

Focus on The Family: http://www.focusonthefamily.com/

From their home page, I found a link to their "Social Issues" page, and from that page, I found another link – especially designed for those who are willing to engage, because from here links are provided for those, "willing to engage even more deeply in legislative and electoral opportunities." This page is at: http://www.focusonthefamily.com/socialissues/how-to-make-a-difference.aspx

Wall Builders – Pro Family Legislative Network: http://profamily.com/aboutus.asp

- ♥ **Street Youth, and helping homeless and street involved youth:**

http://www.streetconnect.org/

While at this site I clicked over to their "Useful Links" page, and found a treasure-trove of links to other organizations – all of which are trying to help homeless and street involved youth, and their parents. This link offers any number of opportunities for those seeking to engage:

http://www.streetconnect.org/useful-links.html

- ♥ **Suicide Prevention:**

National Suicide Prevention Lifeline: http://www.suicidepreventionlifeline.org/GetInvolved/Default.aspx

- ♥ **Teachers Aids:**

How to become a teachers aid - http://www.ehow.com/how_4793741_become-teachers-aid.html

- ♥ **TEENAGERS – WANT TO GET INVOLVED?**

http://rachel-lister.suite101.com/teens-making-a-difference-a14892

I went from this page to another page within their site, where anyone can investigate volunteer opportunities – by your zip code!

http://volunteers.aarp.org/ones/ctg/mansell/registrant/create.htm?language=en&trace=360i2011&CMP=KNC-360I-GOOGLE-CTG&HBX_PK=volunteers&utm_source=GOOGLE&utm_medium=cpc&utm_term=volunteer&utm_campaign=G_Volunteer%2B-%2BContent&360cid=SI_264661869_13061244577_0

♥ **Veteran Organizations in need of assistance:**

Disabled American Veterans -
http://www.dav.org/volunteers/Opportunities.aspx

Military.com offers a link to any number of various Veteran Organizations:
http://www.military.com/spouse/content/military-life/military-resources/military-and-veteran-associations.html

♥ **Virtual Volunteering:**
Volunteer Match has a "Virtual Volunteer" page, where those who are shut-in or unable to volunteer through any other means, may engage in any number of areas needing assistance – ONLINE. This is an outstanding provision for so many talented people who might be Willing To Engage:
http://www.volunteermatch.org/search/index.jsp?v=true

♥ **Volunteering – in general:**
American Red Cross: http://www.redcrossblood.org/volunteer

Salvation Army:
http://www.salvationarmyusa.org/usn/www_usn_2.nsf

Volunteers of America: http://www.voa.org/

Volunteer Match: http://www.volunteermatch.org/

♥ **Volunteering <u>Opportunities for the Handicapped</u>:**
Are YOU in additional need of personal Civil Inspiration?
Watch this U-Tube video from Oklahoma State University:
http://www.youtube.com/watch_popup?v=JVAhr4thZDJE&vq=medium#t=19

♥ **Youth Involvement in Politics:**
http://www.freechild.org/politics.htm
From this page I found dozens of links to other youth oriented
politically based organizations, all striving to educate and motivate
the youth of the world to become politically educated, as well as
politically active.

Although I personally disagree with many of the sites listed and
linked to from this page, I will not edit the offerings of those links.
I can only hope that the youth of our world will learn the reality that
nothing is free, and that we must pay for whatever it is that we
decide to "give to ourselves".

(Thomas Sowell)

"One of the consequences of such notions as
'entitlements' is that people who have contributed
nothing to society feel that society owes them
something, apparently just for being nice enough to
grace us with their presence."

Other Works by
Lawrence T. (Larry) Vosen, Ph.D.

1. "A Diamond on The Wall™"

   "Memoir of the Youngest Green Beret in Vietnam (1967-1968)"

Discussed briefly in our "Author Biography", Larry Vosen entered military service in 1966, at the age of 17. Volunteering to serve in Vietnam, Larry arrived in Southeast Asia at age 18, and was the youngest Green Beret in Vietnam during most of his near-eighteen month tour of duty.

In "A Diamond on The Wall", the true story of how three American Green Berets (of which he was one), along with three of their ARVN (Army of the Republic of Vietnam) counterparts, and one hundred sixty Montagnard Strikers, succeeded in accomplishing what a Battalion of the 4th Division could not do - and in the process, insured that A Diamond on The Wall preceded the name of one fallen American Warrior, and how that recovery mission still impacts his life today.

Copyright 2012, "A Diamond on The Wall" is available for Kindle and Nook, (and other e-Book providers through Amazon.com), and may also be purchased in paperback edition at:

https://www.createspace.com/3769609

2. "The Letters of Faith™"
   www.lettersoffaith.com/

The Letters of Faith are a collection of twenty-four letters (with a concordance), which are directed toward anyone who is seeking to know the truth and fullness of Scripture – and God (Elohim), or having found the basic truth of His Word, who now desire a closer walk with Him.

In use online for almost twenty-four years, The Letters of Faith have been visited by nearly one million readers seeking to find relevancy of life in today's massive dysfunctional society. Evangelistic in part, prophetic in part, and wholly in support of the inerrancy of Scripture, The Letters are an uncompromising exposé on discipleship in a world desperately grasping for love and truth.

3. "The Exalted Name Bible™"
    www.exaltednamebible.com/

The Exalted Name Bible (ENB) is the pinnacle of Dr. Vosen's spiritual contributions and literary accomplishments. Ten Years in the making, the ENB is the ONLY Bible translation available today that contains the full Exalted Name of Elohim (God) throughout its pages.

During the past thirty-three years, Dr. Vosen has been a faithful student of Scripture. Eleven years ago, in the course of preparing a response to a series of questions regarding the Trinity, Dr. Vosen was 'shown' something through Psalm 68:4, which sent him on a quest for knowledge in regard to the "Names" used within current Bible translations. During the course of his quest, Dr. Vosen discovered the truth of the long-lost Exalted Name (which had been replaced by more generic phrases, such as, "The Lord", for instance), and since the moment of that discovery, Dr. Vosen has labored to reinsert THE EXALTED NAME back into Scripture.

The Exalted Name Bible is unlike any other Bible Translation available today, because in reading the fullness of Scripture, in context, and in the full power of The Exalted Name, the Word of Elohim will now leap off the page and into your heart.

Dr. Vosen is pursuing a hard-copy publisher at this time, and with prayer – and the support of our Father in heaven, this task will be accomplished.

4. Scarlet Lace Poems©
   Spiritual Musings

Throughout his career, Dr. Vosen has written a number of very simple and rhythmic poems, which contain an alarming and alluring spiritual depth and insight.

With an insatiable desire to glorify, magnify and exalt our Master, Messiah and King, Dr. Vosen succeeds in accomplishing his goal, while touching on topics such as: abortion, divorce, anger, frustration and even the Gospel message itself.

The Scarlet Lace Poems are an assortment of his most touching and heart-rending works, which we believe will bring joy to your heart for many years to come.

Copyright 2012, Scarlet Lace Poems are available in eBook at Kindle.com, and in paperback at:
https://www.createspace.com/3849880

Made in the USA
Charleston, SC
16 May 2012